THE
TOP
10
most
OUTRAGEOUS
COUPLES
OF THE
BIBLE

AND HOW THEIR STORIES CAN
REVOLUTIONIZE YOUR MARRIAGE

DAVID CLARKE, PH.D.
WITH WILLIAM G. CLARKE, M.A.

SHILOH RUN  PRESS

An Imprint of Barbour Publishing, Inc.

© 2014 by David E. Clarke, PhD

Print ISBN 978-1-68322-857-8

eBook Editions:
Adobe Digital Edition (.epub) 978-1-63058-114-5
Kindle and MobiPocket Edition (.prc) 978-1-63058-115-2

The author is represented by Joyce Hart, Hartline Literary Agency, 123 Queenston Drive, Pittsburgh PA 15235.

Published by Shiloh Run Press, an imprint of Barbour Publishing, Inc., 1810 Barbour Drive, Uhrichsville, Ohio 44683, www.shilohrunpress.com

Our mission is to inspire the world with the life-changing message of the Bible.

Member of the
Evangelical Christian
Publishers Association

Printed in the United States of America.

*To my wonderful parents, Bill and Kathy Clarke,
who have had an outrageous love for over sixty years.*

Contents

Introduction

OUTRAGEOUS IS A BEAUTIFUL THING

> **out·ra·geous** \ aut-'ra-jes\ *adj* **1 a:** exceeding the limits of what is usual **b:** not conventional or matter-of-fact : FANTASTIC **2:** VIOLENT, UNRESTRAINED **3 a:** going beyond all standards of what is right or decent[1]

I love outrageous. Why? Because outrageous is never boring. You simply can't overlook it. You can't ignore it. It gets in your face and seizes your attention. It's intense. It's vibrant. It radiates drama and excitement. It's very entertaining. It's unforgettable.

It's not always pretty, but it's always powerful. It has impact.

Be honest. Would you have picked up a book titled *The Top 10 Nice Couples of the Bible*? or *The Top 10 Stable Couples of the Bible*? I doubt it.

The best thing about outrageous is that it is a fantastic teacher. Especially when it comes to male-female romantic relationships. I refer to certain couples as *outrageous couples*. These couples demonstrate, in compelling and memorable ways, what does *not* work and what *does* work in opposite-sex relationships.

> **out·ra·geous** \ aut-'ra-jes\ **couples** \ 'kəp-əls\ *n* **1 a:** well outside what is typical **b:** not routine or run-of-the-mill : ZANY **2:** SHOCKING, UNCONVENTIONAL **3:** when they're bad, they're very bad; but when they're good, they're very, very good[2]

---

[1] *Webster's New Collegiate Dictionary* (Springfield, MA: G. & C. Merriam Co., 1977).
[2] Definition based on the professional experience of Dr. David E. Clarke.

Outrageous couples don't just make mistakes. They make huge, messy mistakes that lead to terrible and lasting damage in their relationships. When we observe the disastrous consequences of this seriously bad behavior, we are deeply motivated to avoid making the same horrendous choices.

It's also true that outrageous couples make good choices—and not just good choices but wonderful, extremely positive choices that lead to significant and lasting rewards in their relationships. When we observe the rich payoffs of this seriously positive behavior, we are intensely inspired to replicate those excellent choices.

This is dynamic learning by example.

As a practicing psychologist for more than twenty years, I've worked with a lot of outrageous couples. Nice, normal couples tend not to show up in my office. Here is a sampling of outrageous couples I've seen in marital therapy.

THE UNDERWEAR ATTACKER

The wife had a hair-trigger temper and would launch into massive tirades when her husband didn't meet her needs. She gave new meaning to the term "drama queen." He was a quiet, passive, and introverted man. One of her favorite motivational techniques was to wait until he had backed his car into the street to go to work in the morning. Then she'd run out in front of the vehicle, yelling and waving her arms like a crazy woman. She did this while dressed only in a bra and panties. It was very entertaining for the neighbors, and she usually got what she wanted from her embarrassed husband.

THE POOPER SCOOPERS

Both were professionals. Bright, successful, well dressed, and sophisticated. They also had been engaged in a five-year battle over who scooped the most dog poop from their beautifully manicured front lawn. It was an ongoing weekly contest. "I scooped thirty-eight piles of poop this past week, you slacker!" "Oh, yeah? I scooped forty piles of poop, and I've got the evidence to prove it!"

I told them they had two choices: Get rid of their dogs, or grow up, stop fighting a mere symptom, and start dealing with their *real* issues.

THE NUDIST

The very conservative, prim and proper wife whispered to me: "My husband suddenly doesn't want me to wear clothes. He walks around the home completely naked." He grinned broadly and said, "That's right! Being naked feels wonderful and natural. I can be who I really am. I've been visiting a nudist retreat on the weekends, and I want my wife to come with me." I thought to myself: *What you really are is a nutball!* I told this guy he had a problem, and if he didn't fix it and get his clothes back on, he'd be a very lonely naked man.

THE BOGUS WAR HERO

The husband said he was a Vietnam veteran who suffered from post-traumatic stress disorder. He told a detailed story of an ambush in which he fought off the enemy almost single-handedly. Weeping, he said that near the end of the firefight, his close buddy was killed in front of him. Turned out, he wasn't a Vietnam veteran. In fact, his wife discovered he had never been in any branch of the military. Not surprisingly, he had lied about a lot of other things as well.

ADULTERY AT ITS WORST

Sobbing, the wife told me that she had just found out that her husband had been having sex with her best friend. It had been going on for about a year. But that wasn't all. The husband and his mistress had been having sex while the wife was in her room sleeping. Her friend would visit and stay up late "talking" with her husband. It was a double betrayal, and it was devastating.

SHE WHO IS ALWAYS RIGHT

Once the wife gave her opinion on a subject—any subject—that was the final word. She was right, and she demanded that her husband accept *the* truth and agree with her. She could not stand for him to disagree with her on anything. If he tried to hold to his point of view, she'd have a fit: crying, screaming, moaning, foaming at the mouth, and throwing herself on the floor. This behavior would continue until the husband gave in and agreed with her. The poor man wasn't even allowed to believe that one kind of mustard was the best unless it was her favorite too.

You Ain't Seen Nothin' Yet

I could go on and on. I've learned a great deal about relationships from all the outrageous couples I've seen in my therapy office. And, frankly, I've enjoyed every minute of it. But in terms of sheer outrageousness, my therapy couples can't hold a candle to some of the couples in the Bible.

God could certainly have chosen to feature only couples who were solid, dependable, and balanced. He didn't do that. He did just the opposite. I don't think He could have selected a more dysfunctional, mixed-up, unbalanced, and volatile group of couples. Even the few consistently healthy couples in the Bible live lives that are extraordinary and way outside the norm. The ten biblical couples highlighted in this book aren't even close to typical:

- History's first sinners, who changed marriage forever
- A stupid playboy and his manipulative, conniving main squeeze
- A mean-as-a-snake, abusive husband and his faithful wife
- The world's worst parents
- Two mismatched partners who refused to quit on their marriage
- Passionate lovers who prove you can be married and still enjoy sizzling romance and sex
- The ultimate hedonists, whose love for pleasure destroyed them
- A selfish coward and his cynical, blame-everybody-else wife

- A too-good-to-be-true wife and her very happy husband
- A couple who stuck together and clung to God through extremely traumatic circumstances

I wasn't kidding when I told you these folks were outrageous. These ten couples didn't do anything in a low-key, ho-hum way. When they made mistakes, they made nightmarish mistakes that cost them dearly. When they made good choices, they made spectacularly good choices that transformed their relationships.

The Top Ten and What They Can Teach Us

What's fascinating to me is that these ten couples are not outrageous for the sake of being outrageous. God doesn't tell the stories for their entertainment value—though they are very entertaining. God included the stories of these couples in the Bible because they can teach us vital relationship lessons.

These top ten couples teach us, quite literally, how to build a great marriage. They teach other spiritual principles as well, but they certainly teach a complete set of marital truths. If all we had were these ten couples and their stories, we'd have all the information needed to create an outrageously *great* marriage.

Get Ready for One Wild Ride

In Part One, we study four couples whose relationships contain both outrageously *bad* and outrageously *good* behavior: Adam and Eve; Abraham and Sarah; Jacob, Leah, and Rachel; and Solomon and Shulamith.

In Part Two, we'll focus on four couples whose relationships contained only outrageously *bad* behavior: Lot and his wife, Isaac and Rebekah, Samson and Delilah, and Nabal and Abigail.

In Part Three, we'll zero in on two couples whose relationships contained only outrageously *good* behavior: the Proverbs 31 wife and her husband, and Joseph and Mary.

I hope you're ready for a wild-and-fun ride through the

lives of these ten couples. When we're done, you'll have the tools you need to avoid relationship disaster, and you'll be equipped to make your own marriage all you've ever wanted it to be.

Hang on. Here we go.

Outrageous Interaction

1. Think of a couple you know who made outrageously *bad* choices. What damage and pain did they cause themselves and others? Did they recover and restore their marriage?

2. Think of a couple you know who made outrageously *good* choices. What rewards and benefits did they earn for themselves and others? Which of their good choices would you most like to emulate?

3. Before you and your spouse met and became a couple, what was one outrageously *bad* choice you made, and what was its cost?

4. Before you and your spouse met and became a couple, what was one outrageously *good* choice you made, and what was its positive impact?

5. Discuss any outrageously *good* choices you each have made so far in your relationship (other than choosing to be together—which was obviously a terrific choice!). What positives have resulted from these excellent choices?

PART ONE

THE BAD AND THE GOOD

Adam and Eve

Outrageous Sin
and Spiritual Bonding

1.
You've Got to Team Up against Sin

A man and a woman are walking together in the cool of the day in a beautiful, lush garden. As the sun sets, the breeze feels good, and the temperature is just right. As they walk along hand in hand, this married couple communicates in an open, honest, and personal way.

Both the husband and the wife spontaneously express their thoughts, emotions, needs, and reactions. They hold nothing back. They have no secrets from each other. There are no obstacles or problems to overcome in communication.

The man and woman are totally in sync with each other. They are completely satisfied and fulfilled in every aspect of their relationship. Every time they talk, they achieve deep and connected emotional intimacy. Every time they make love, they enjoy magnificent physical passion. Every time they talk to God as a couple, they experience a powerful spiritual bond.

Their minds are in tune. Their bodies are in tune. Their souls are in tune.

They live every day in joyful oneness in the presence of God. In fact, God is with them now as they walk in the garden. As if to symbolize their unique bond of closeness, the man and the woman have no clothes on. They are completely naked, and they are not ashamed.

Who am I talking about? I'm happy to tell you that this couple is my dear wife, Sandy, and me. On a recent vacation to the garden island of Kauai in the Hawaiian Islands, we decided to take it all off and stroll through a lush, secluded area at sunset. It was fantastic. . .until we came face-to-face with a group of about twenty tourists. That was unfortunate.

All right. I can't go any further. I'm kidding. This couple is not Sandy and me. We've never even been to Kauai. The last time we walked in a garden, it was in Portland, Oregon, and we had a fight. I got tired of all the roses and wanted to go get a steak dinner.

Don't get me wrong. We have a great marriage, and we're always working to improve it. But it's not as great as the marriage I've described. So, no, it's not Sandy and me. And it's not you and your spouse either. Do you know any couple who has it this fantastic? This perfect? I doubt it.

Well, who are these outrageous people? They are Adam and Eve! (You knew that, didn't you?) They were history's first couple, and they had it good. Really, really good. Read Genesis 2:23–25 and tell me what kind of relationship they enjoyed:

> *The man said, "This is now bone of my bones, and flesh of my flesh; she shall be called Woman, because she was taken out of Man." For this reason a man shall leave his father and his mother, and be joined to his wife; and they shall become one flesh. And the man and his wife were both naked and were not ashamed.*

Wow! I mean, *wow*! Adam and Eve experienced the kind of incredible closeness and vulnerability that most couples can only dream about. I especially like the part about being naked and unashamed. That sounds like fun!

GETTING A GARDEN OF EDEN LOVE

Do you want what Adam and Eve had? I know you do. Me too. I firmly believe that every married couple can achieve an Adam and Eve, Garden of Eden love relationship. It won't be exactly what Adam and Eve had, but it will be very close.

How do you get a Garden of Eden love? First, by buying

this book. You've done that. Good job. (That will help me pay for my children's college education.) Second, by studying—and learning from—the relationship mistakes and successes of the ten outrageous couples in this book. These ten couples reveal all you need to know about creating your own outrageously great marriage, the kind of marriage enjoyed by Adam and Eve before the Fall.

HOW TO AVOID SERIOUS MARITAL SIN

Adam and Eve had it all. And all they had to do to keep it was obey God's command not to eat the fruit from one tree in this beautiful Garden of Eden (Genesis 2:16–17). Pretty easy, right? Wrong! They ate the fruit from that tree, committing the world's first human sin. An outrageously bad sin. Their marriage, and every other marriage that followed, was forever changed by that decision.

The devastating results of their sin are recorded in Genesis 3:6–24. The two worst consequences of the incalculably tragic fallout were that they were separated from God and from each other. They lost their oneness. Before they sinned, their "differentness" had been irrelevant to them; they were equal before God and felt no competitiveness. Immediately after they sinned, their differences were all they could see, and in shame they covered their nakedness (Genesis 3:7).

They also lost their connection with God, the blessed communion and friendship they had enjoyed with their loving Creator (Genesis 3:8–10). These losses were so great that they are beyond comprehension. Far beyond the effects of this original sin on *marriage* were the consequences that Adam's sin brought to the entire human race: estrangement from God, suffering, disease, death, and all the troubles of the world.

Couples today suffer the same terrible consequences—loss of oneness, amplified differences, shame—as a result of serious marital sin. I use the term "marital sin" because, when you're married, every sin you commit affects both you and your spouse. Let me be clear: *All* marital sin, no matter how seemingly small or horribly large, is serious and has profound consequences. But there are certain marital sins that are particularly damaging—sins that the Bible calls *grievous*.

Clearly, there is a world of difference between not doing a household chore and choosing not to work when you are fully capable of holding a job and supporting your spouse and family. Between the occasional insensitive comment and a pattern of vicious verbal abuse. Between a few extra hours of overtime and chronic workaholism. Between forgetting flowers on Valentine's Day and committing adultery.

I want you to strive to avoid all marital sins. But my focus here is on avoiding serious marital sins, because these sins do deep, far-reaching harm. That's what I am writing about in this chapter.

Every spouse has an area of potential serious sin, an area of weakness that can cause terrible damage to the marriage. Maybe your sin is still in the "potential" zone and hasn't yet fully developed and severely damaged your marriage. Maybe your sin has blown past the potential stage and is a monster that has already wreaked havoc on your spouse and your marriage. Either way, the time to address your sin—in a new and effective way—is *now*.

You know what your weakness is. Maybe it's pornography. Lack of interest in sex with your spouse. Paying attention to men or women who are not your spouse. Not spending enough happy time with your spouse. Selfish preoccupation with your activities. Work. Food. Spending. Alcohol. Drugs. Verbal abuse. Physical abuse. Clamming up and not communicating. Gambling. Controlling. Being a doormat and allowing your spouse to walk all over you. Spiritual apathy and indifference. Being too tough on your kids. Not being tough enough on your kids. Being too focused on your kids. I think you get the idea.

There's someone else who knows your weaknesses. Satan. And just as he did with Adam and Eve, Satan will do everything in his considerable power to entice you toward your serious sin. As your marriage suffers from your sin—whether still in secret or exposed—Satan will be laughing his evil head off.

Adam and Eve's downfall in Genesis 3 teaches us *how to avoid serious marital sin*. By examining the process of how they sinned, you can discover how to interrupt and disrupt the process you go through on the way to your serious sin. Not sinning in a serious way is a vital step toward having an outrageously great marriage.

STEP ONE: THE TEMPTATION

Satan's temptation of Eve (Genesis 3:1–6) contains all the essential elements of every temptation: questioning God's word; denying God's word; believing the lie that the sin will give us something much better than what God will give us for obeying His commands; and being tempted in our area of weakness. (The very first adjective used to describe Satan in the Bible is here in Genesis 3: *crafty*, which also means clever or cunning.)

STEP TWO: THE RATIONALIZATION

With Satan's help, Eve rationalizes her sin. She tells herself: *There will be no negative consequences; my behavior will meet my deepest needs; and I will experience intense pleasure.* All these rationalizations are lies, but Satan is a master of convincing us otherwise. He has always been a liar (John 8:44), as he was with Eve, and he comes to us not as he really is but disguised as "an angel of light" (2 Corinthians 11:14).

STEP THREE: THE CHOICE TO SIN

Because Eve chose to believe Satan's lies in the temptation and rationalization steps, she was doomed when the time came to decide whether to sin. Her mind was already made up, and her natural desire for the fruit pushed her over the edge.

STEP FOUR: THE CONSEQUENCES

After Adam and Eve sinned, Satan's statements were exposed as lies, and the consequences struck home with terrible force. I believe the worst consequence was *separation*: from God

(Genesis 3:8) and from each other (Genesis 3:7).

What is most striking to me in Adam and Eve's sin process is that they were *together* the entire time (Genesis 3:6). When Satan tempted Eve, Adam was right by her side or not far away. When Eve rationalized her sin, qualifying her disobedience as good and right, Adam was right by her side. When Eve sinned by eating the fruit, Adam was right by her side. In fact, Mr. Supportive was complicit in his wife's sin and ate the fruit as well.

Whatever happened to teamwork? I'll tell you what happened. *Adam and Eve didn't talk to each other as they marched closer and closer to their sin.* It is probable that not one word was uttered between them. They were the only people on earth, and yet they didn't talk! Teamwork, especially teamwork against Satan, is only effective when a couple *communicates*.

Without honest communication, your sin will zoom past the potential stage to the devastating impact stage. It's only a matter of time.

With open and honest communication, Adam and Eve could have battled Satan and won. They could have avoided this disastrous sin and become closer to each other and to God. If Eve had asked for Adam's help and he had spoken truth to her, Satan would have slithered away in humiliating defeat.

Eve: Adam, this serpent says that God told us we can't eat from *any* tree in the garden. God didn't say that, did He?

Adam: You know He didn't. God said we can eat from all the trees *except one*.

Eve: That's what I told the serpent—that we can't eat from or touch the tree in the center of the garden.

Adam: Honey, what you just said isn't true. God didn't say we would die if we *touched* the tree, only if we *ate* from it. Why did you change what God said? The serpent is getting to you, isn't he?

Eve:	The serpent is making some good points. What if the serpent is right, and we won't die if we eat the fruit? What if—as he has told me—we can be like God when we eat it? What if the serpent is right and God is not being good and fair to us in telling us we can't eat from that one tree?
Adam:	Eve, listen to yourself! You know what God told us. We will die if we eat it. The serpent is a dirty liar. He's calling God a liar. Who are you going to believe? God, who created us and gave us this beautiful garden and a fantastic life together, or this stupid, malevolent serpent, who is lying his head off?
Eve:	But, Adam, the fruit looks good, and I think it will be delicious. And I believe it will give us special wisdom. Why can't we exercise our free will?
Adam:	Eve, have you lost your mind? Now I know why I've always hated snakes. You are buying the serpent's pack of lies. He's attractive and clever and persuasive, but he's an evil liar. Take my hand, and let's get out of here. We're going to tell God right now what this dirtball creature is up to. I'll bet God kicks the serpent out of the garden, and I want to see it.

A REVOLUTIONARY IDEA FOR MARRIAGE

I'm going to recommend something that will scare you.

It's something that 99 percent of couples do not have. It's something that the Christian community doesn't talk about. It's also something that will protect you from serious marital sin and give you a deep level of intimacy.

What I want you to have—and what I'm convinced God

wants you to have—is a *wide-open, vulnerable marriage.* A marriage characterized by complete and total honesty about your individual areas of weakness.

That's right. I'm urging you to reveal to each other the sinful behaviors that Satan is most likely to tempt you to do. It's time to talk about your sins, whether they are still in the potential stage or in full destructive mode.

No more secrets. No more covering up. No more denial. No more lies.

In many cases, your sin is obvious, and your spouse knows exactly what it is. In other cases, your sin is secret, and your spouse has no idea what you're doing. Whether your sin is out in the open or hidden, sit down with your spouse and disclose everything you know about your damaging behavior. When it started. Why you think it started. The unresolved past pain that may be the power source of your sin. What, specifically, you have done up to now in your area of sin. Give the details.

Identify the current triggers that set you on the path to doing your sin. Talk about how Satan goes about tempting you to sin. Discuss the rationalizations you use to excuse and justify your sin. Go over why you continue to sin in this area. What does it do for you? What are the payoffs? What needs are you trying to meet?

Talk about your guilt and shame. Admit that you're wrong and you're very sorry for your sin and the pain it has caused God and your spouse and your family. Describe the damage your sin has done to you, your relationship with God, and your marriage.

Allow—even *invite*—your spouse to vent all feelings about your sin and its impact on your marriage. Allow your spouse to ask as many questions as necessary to form a complete picture of your sinful behavior. Healing and the beginning of trust will come through many private conversations about your sin.

Ask for your spouse's ongoing help in dealing with your sinful behavior pattern. Commit to telling your spouse anytime you are seriously tempted to sin in your area of weakness. Commit

to telling your spouse whenever you are beginning the rationalization process on the way to your sin. *You know* when you're in
real trouble.

Thinking of acts that would dishonor God, your marriage,
and your Christian testimony and would bring anguish to your
spouse is where sin originates, long before you take action to
commit your sin. Jesus emphasized this: "For out of the heart
[the desires, the mind] come evil thoughts, murders, adul-
teries, fornications, thefts, false witness, slanders" (Matthew
15:19). Long before Peter denied Him, Jesus rebuked Peter
with these words: "Get behind Me, Satan! You are a stumbling
block to Me; for you are not setting your mind on God's interests, but man's" (Matthew 16:23). The apostle Paul emphasized
the importance of the mind in leading us either toward or away
from sin (Romans 8:5-7; 12:1-2), and he told the Philippian
believers and the church at Colossae how to *set* their minds on
things that would draw them away from sin (Philippians 4:7-8;
Colossians 3:2).

Agree with your spouse that, at the point of heavy-duty
temptation or rationalization, you will call him or her *before*
you act out your desire to sin. If necessary, you will wake him
or her out of a sound sleep. You will share the struggle you are
having with your sin. In response, your spouse agrees to speak
the truth in a loving way. He or she will support you and give
you added strength to gain the victory over your temptation.
Agree with your spouse that the two of you will pray together
and ask for God's help when tempted. It will be the two of
you and God against Satan (Ecclesiastes 4:9-12; Matthew
18:19-20).

I'm not suggesting that you reveal to your spouse every
temptation or sinful thought that comes into your mind. That
would drive both of you crazy. But when you are really struggling with temptation or recurrent thoughts that persist, and
you are in real danger of acting out those thoughts, *that's when
you tell your spouse what's happening.*

Keep in mind, it's not going to be just one of you being

totally honest about your area of sin. It's going to be *both* of you, because both of you have an area of potential serious sin. That's why you support *each other*. You *pray* for each other. You hold each other accountable.

You may need another accountability partner, a friend of the same sex. You may need a Christian therapist. You may need a Christ-centered addiction group such as Celebrate Recovery. But your most important teammate and accountability partner in your ongoing battle against your sinful behavior pattern is always going to be your spouse.

You've Got to Be Kidding!

Are you freaking out yet? Are you feeling massive anxiety? Are you thinking, *What are you, nuts? I can't tell my spouse the details of my sinful behavior and give an update every time I'm in serious temptation mode. That's way too personal! I'll just handle it myself. It's also risky. The truth will hurt my spouse terribly and may even lead to a separation or divorce. Our marriage will never be the same.*

If you're thinking this way, join the club. Every couple to whom I've recommended my *wide-open, vulnerable marriage* plan has voiced these same protests. Here are my answers.

First, what happened to Adam and Eve because they did not communicate openly and honestly on the way to their sins? They sinned, and the results of their sin were cataclysmic, not only for their marriage but for the entire human race.

Second, if you do not join your spouse in battling your temptation to sin, you'll continue to sin. You cannot handle it on your own. Your sin will end up handling you. Your sin will severely damage your marriage and could lead to a separation or divorce. The divorce rate among Christian couples, those who say they know Jesus personally, is about 50 percent. This is the same rate as among non-Christian couples. Isn't it time for a different approach?

Third, even if your spouse never discovers your sin—which is very unlikely—the cover-up and secrets will separate you from each other. It will always be a black hole between you. Secrets separate. The truth connects.

Fourth, when your sins are on the table, and you're working as a sin-defeating team, you will create amazing intimacy. Talking about your feelings of temptation to sin and sins you are committing or have committed is incredibly personal and connects couples on a deep level. If you can talk about your temptations and sins, you can talk about anything. And you will! Your openness about your sinful patterns will spread to every other area of your lives, and your communication will reach levels you never dreamed possible.

The Workaholic and the Momma

I don't recommend strategies that Sandy and I don't do ourselves. I'm a workaholic. Sandy focuses too much on our four kids. These are our main areas of potential serious sin.

If I had not curtailed my work habits with Sandy's help, my marriage would have been ruined. If Sandy had not, with my help, learned to put me above the children, terrible damage would have been done to our marriage. Over time, these habits would have done just as much damage to our marriage as adultery, alcoholism, verbal abuse, or other more "dramatic" sins.

We continue to work as a team to help each other avoid sinning in these areas. By working together in honesty, we have been able to largely control these behaviors, and our teamwork has produced a wonderful intimacy. Workaholism and overemphasis on the kids remain a struggle, but as a one-flesh team, we overcome them every day.

I have helped hundreds of couples join forces against their areas of weakness and sin. It is a huge part of my therapy with every couple I see. It is not an easy process, because honesty and vulnerability do not come naturally to most people. But it is a process that results in a strong, sin-avoiding, and intimate one-flesh partnership.

If serious sin has already devastated your relationship, teaming up with openness and honesty can lead to complete healing and restoration. *Together* you can stay away from further damaging sin in that area. If serious sin has not yet ravaged your marriage, you can keep your potentially serious sin at bay and protect your marriage by becoming a team *now*.

Learn from Adam and Eve's shocking lack of teamwork. Have the guts to step out in faith and become teammates in fighting your sins. You'll regret it if you don't. You'll never regret it if you do.

It may seem like an outrageous idea, but I believe it is an outrageously good idea.

Outrageous Interaction

1. Name some areas in your marriage in which you have been a good team. What were the benefits of this teamwork?

2. Name some areas in your marriage in which you have *not* been a good team. What were the negative results of not playing on the same side as teammates in these areas?

3. It's nitty-gritty time. Tell your spouse about the areas in which you are prone to sin. If your area of weakness has not yet caused damage, describe to your spouse the damage it could cause. Ask your spouse to describe to you the damage your potential sin could cause.

4. If your sin has already caused serious damage—to yourself, your spouse, your family, and to God—describe the damage you've done. Ask your spouse to describe to you the damage your sin has caused.

5. Agree that you will work as a team against your sins. Agree to tell your spouse immediately when you are seriously tempted by Satan in your area of weakness. Ask for your spouse's support in battling your potential for sin.

6. Pray briefly right now that God will come alongside you as a couple and give you power to defeat your sins.

2.
The Secret to Being Soul Mates

Think of the most wonderful times you've ever had as a couple. Those times are not hard to recall, are they? They are truly unforgettable. Unusual closeness. Powerful feelings of love. A special intimacy. Deep emotional, physical, and spiritual connection. Oneness.

I call these times *peak couple experiences*.

THE LOVE BOAT CRUISE

Two years ago, Sandy and I had a four-day peak couple experience when we took a cruise to celebrate our twenty-fifth wedding anniversary. It was a magical time for us. No distractions. No responsibilities. No bills. It was a successful escape from life and into our relationship.

No kids either. Kids don't belong on a cruise ship. They belong at home, far away from you and not bothering anyone else. Our four kids tried to get on the ship. But they didn't make it. As our ship pulled out, we could see them running down the dock and waving their arms. We waved goodbye and went to the other side of the ship.

We loved everything about the cruise. Stress-free relaxation. Eating. Reading by the pool. Eating. Walking on the promenade deck hand in hand. Eating. Enjoying the ship entertainment. Eating. The only negative part of the cruise was that we couldn't eat more food.

Our lovemaking was incredible. Even better than the eating. Our unbelievably tiny room had only a bed and a bathroom. All it was good for was making love. . .and that's what we did. When the cruise was over and it was time to leave the ship, I locked myself in the room and refused to come out. I told the captain and his security officers: "You don't understand. I've been making love to my beautiful wife every day in this cabin! More than once a day! I'm not leaving. We're going to live on this ship!"

The best part of the cruise was being together all the time. Talking, laughing, and touching. Sandy is my favorite person in the world, and having her all to myself was fantastic. We were in our own perfect little world of closeness, intimacy, and love.

Sandy and I have had other peak couple experiences. Our wedding day. The honeymoon night. Actually, the entire honeymoon week. Our whirlwind day in San Francisco a few years ago after one of my marriage seminars. Getaway weekends at the beach in Clearwater, Florida. Long walks on the beach at sunset.

"I WANT MORE!"

I know you've also had peak couple experiences. You've been remembering them as you've read the last few paragraphs. They were terrific, weren't they? Don't you wish you could have more of them? A lot more?

The problem with peak couple experiences is that there aren't that many of them. They are mind-blowingly wonderful, but they don't happen very often, and they don't last very long. Peak couple experiences almost always occur during vacations, when you're away from home and kids. When you return home, the reality of life immediately smacks you in the kisser, and your peak experience ends with a thud.

What if I told you there is a way for you to enjoy many more peak couple experiences? What if I told you that you can have one or two peak couple experiences a week? Wouldn't that be great? Wouldn't that deepen your love relationship and bring the two of you much closer? You know it would.

The secret to dramatically increasing the number of your peak couple experiences is found in the story of Adam and Eve.

BEFORE THEIR SIN, ADAM AND EVE WALKED WITH GOD

When Adam and Eve were in the Garden of Eden and hadn't sinned yet, they lived in perfect harmony with each other and with God. They were as intimate as two individuals can be. You just don't get any closer than "bone of my bones, and flesh of my flesh" (Genesis 2:23).

Every day was a peak couple experience!

Why were Adam and Eve so happy and so close to each other? Because *God was at the center* of their relationship. Genesis 2:24 describes their relationship as "one flesh." This means they were completely connected in the three areas of intimacy: physical, emotional, and spiritual. Since the Bible teaches that the spiritual is the most important part of us as persons, the spiritual must also be the most important part of us as couples.

It was not Adam and Eve in the Garden of Eden. It was Adam and Eve and God in the Garden of Eden. God was the most important part of their lives and their relationship. Living in His presence and being "one flesh" spiritually gave them unlimited joy and closeness.

AFTER THEIR SIN, ADAM AND EVE WALKED WITH GOD

When they disobeyed God, Adam and Eve broke their one-flesh bond. Immediately, they were separated from God and from each other. *When they lost their intimate connection with God*, they automatically lost their intimate connection with each other. Suddenly, they experienced something they had never felt and never believed they would feel: they were afraid of God! Instead of thrilling to His presence, they *hid* from Him (Genesis 3:8–10).

Even though God laid serious consequences on them (Genesis 3:16–19) and banished them from their perfect environment (Genesis 3:23–24), He allowed and even encouraged Adam and Eve to mount a comeback. Their comeback was fueled by God and His continued love for them. God still wanted to be at the center of their relationship.

God let Adam and Eve live; and He didn't give up on them. His tender love is evident in what He did for them after they sinned:

> *The LORD God made garments of skin for Adam and his wife, and clothed them.*
>
> GENESIS 3:21

What a gentle, sweet, and undeserved act of love! God still loved and cared for Adam and Eve. He would continue to be the One who provided for their needs.

Adam and Eve's comeback as a couple was successful because they renewed their relationship and fellowship with God and again put Him at the center of their lives. Eve's statement of praise to God for her firstborn son (Genesis 4:1) shows she was back in a solid, close relationship with the Lord. Abel's faith in God (Genesis 4:4) indicates that he was raised by parents who taught him the priority of obeying God.

KEEP GOD AT THE CENTER OF YOUR RELATIONSHIP

I believe Adam and Eve teach us that true intimacy and happiness in marriage are created when we keep God at the center of our lives and our relationships. *Before they sinned*, God was at the center of their relationship, and they enjoyed a fantastic love relationship. *After they sinned*, God was back at the center of their relationship. That was the key to their comeback.

My point? If you want a terrific marriage and many peak couple experiences, you must keep God at the center of your relationship. If you keep God at the edge of your marriage, on the outside, you have zero chance of building a genuinely great relationship. You'll be doing marriage on your own, and that always leads to disaster. I hope you've learned that lesson by now. It took Sandy and me years to learn it.

BE SPIRITUALLY INTIMATE AS A COUPLE

You keep God at the center of your relationship by *being spiritually intimate* on a regular basis. When you are spiritually intimate, God's power and presence operate at full strength in your marriage. You and your spouse no longer love each other in human strength alone. God Himself does the loving *through* you. He will work in and through both of you to produce the best and deepest love possible on earth.

Joining spiritually is the secret to genuine, lasting intimacy in marriage. I call this spiritual bonding. Spiritual bonding comes by consistently placing God at the very hub of your marriage and growing ever closer to Him as a couple.

Here's how to get started on your adventure of spiritual bonding.

YOU BOTH MUST BE CHRISTIANS

To bond spiritually, both husband and wife must be spiritually alive (Ephesians 2:1, 5). That means both must be Christians. A Christian is someone who has a personal relationship with the one true God, the God of the Bible, through His Son, Jesus Christ.

The only way to God is through Jesus (John 14:6; Acts 4:12). God sent Jesus to die for your sins, to sacrifice His life so that you could have a relationship with God: "For God so loved the world, that He gave His only begotten Son, that whoever believes in Him shall not perish, but have eternal life" (John 3:16). As the apostle Paul establishes in 1 Corinthians 15:3–4, our relationship with God and our ability to know Him in a personal way are built on three central truths: Christ died for our sins in accordance with the Scriptures; He was buried; and He was raised on the third day.

If you have never made the decision to believe that Jesus died and rose from the dead, you can do it right now by saying the words in this brief prayer:

> *Dear God,*
> *I know I am a sinner. I've made many mistakes in my*
> *life. I realize that my sin separates me from You, a*
> *holy God.*
> *I believe that Your Son, Jesus Christ, died for my sins,*
> *was buried, and rose from the dead.*
> *I give my life to You now.*

If you're not ready yet to become a Christian, I still recommend strongly that you and your spouse begin a spiritual bonding process. And I pray that, along the way, you will come to know God through Jesus.

The Husband Needs to Lead

God's design for marriage, as expressed in Ephesians 5:22–24, is for the husband to lead his wife in every area of their relationship, including the spiritual aspect. Of course, the wife is fully involved in spiritual bonding. It's reciprocal. But, husband, you are responsible for making sure that two essential keys to spiritual bonding happen on a regular basis: *prayer* and *spiritual conversations.*

Ask a solid, happily married Christian man to hold you accountable in this area of spiritual leadership. If you can find a man who is leading his wife spiritually, sign him up immediately as your mentor and accountability partner. This could be your pastor, an older man in the church, or a friend around your age.

Your wife will be thrilled with your spiritual leadership. Trust me. Your marriage will improve dramatically. You'll be modeling for your kids how to build a Christian marriage. Best of all, God will be pleased, and He will bless you.

How to Pray

You can pray as a couple in many different, creative ways. The following practical guidelines can get you started:

Start small. Meaningful times of prayer don't have to be long and drawn-out. I suggest a very doable five minutes for starters. The point is to establish a regular habit of praying together. Over time, how long you pray will take care of itself. I always recommend that couples start with at least four prayer times per week. (So, a total of twenty minutes per week—everyone can find time for that.) And here's the important part: No kids. No television. No phones. Just the two of you sitting down in a private place to pray. This not only makes prayer more convenient but also creates a deeper mood and warms you up for spiritual conversations (which we'll discuss next).

Choose a special place in your home to pray. Find a regular place to pray that is private, quiet, and conducive to conversation. Get the kids out of your hair. This is not family devotions;

it's couple prayer time.

When you pray, hold hands. This connects you and is an outward expression of your one-flesh relationship.

Pray out loud. You're not spiritually bonding if you pray silently. Hearing your partner talk to God is an important part of sharing his or her bond with God. If one spouse struggles with praying out loud, he or she can pray silently for the first few times. But the goal is to break the ice and establish a foundation of spiritual intimacy. That can only happen if both spouses are willing to take the risk and pray out loud with each other.

Maybe you feel intimidated about praying in front of your spouse because you think he or she talks better than you and probably prays better than you. The truth is, we all learn how to pray by praying. There's nothing to be embarrassed about. Your spouse will never criticize your prayers. More likely, he or she will be happy and impressed beyond words that you're praying together.

Most likely, in the beginning, neither you nor your spouse will pray on a deep, personal level. You'll bring up topics that are important but not especially deep or intimate. As you become comfortable with the process, gradually increase your transparency in prayer.

Make a list, and take turns in prayer. Before you start to pray, take a minute or two to jot down the requests you each want to bring before God. (Husband, here's a small opportunity to take the lead by having pen and paper ready.) When you have a list, divide it between you and pray one at a time. Here's a list of categories to cover in your prayer times:

- known needs of family, friends, and neighbors;
- your kids—their hearts, their futures, their friendships, their relationship with God, their school experience;
- issues at work—for husband or wife;
- issues at home—for the wife, who is either a stay-at-home mom or is juggling work and home responsibilities;

- your marriage—but, at least initially, don't pray for "issues" in the marriage; instead, pray for closeness, being of one mind, finding time for each other, finding time for prayer and conversation. Pray for God to make Himself real to your spouse.

Your prayer list will also serve as a written record of God's faithfulness. As God answers your prayers, jot down the answers and the date when God gave you that answer.

As you continue to pray together, you'll find that you'll both be more open and personal in what you say to God. You'll pray for your real concerns and the deep desires of your hearts. You'll share intimate things that you would never share in front of any other person.

HOW TO HAVE SPIRITUAL CONVERSATIONS

I always recommend that couples schedule four half-hour "Couple Talk Times" per week. (You'll be surprised by how quickly thirty minutes pass once you start doing this.) Again, no kids, no phones, no TV. Find a place that is comfortable, quiet, and conducive to conversation. You can spend part of your scheduled Couple Talk Times talking about spiritual things. Most married couples don't do this, and they miss out on some wonderful spiritual bonding. The spiritual aspect of your life and your relationship is the most important part, so sharing it will create some pretty intense intimacy. Probably even some passion. Would you like some intimacy and passion? Talk spiritually on a regular basis. Here's a brief list of spiritual topics you can talk about as a couple:

- How God guided you today
- How God blessed you today
- A verse you read this morning
- How you're doing spiritually right now
- How you're struggling with God and why
- What God said to you through the pastor's sermon

- How God wants you to apply the sermon
- How God wants you to serve in the church
- How your service in the church is going
- What you're learning in your personal devotions
- How God wants you to share Christ with your neighbor
- How Satan was all over you today and what happened
- How God is testing you at your job

What we're talking about here is *discipleship*. When you talk and learn together, you are discipling each other! You can help your spouse grow spiritually. Your marriage ought to be the most important discipling relationship in your life. It can be if you begin to talk spiritually.

"ARE WE READY FOR SPIRITUAL BONDING?"

This spiritual bonding idea is a lot to take in, isn't it? I know it's tough to get your heads around it. It will be a risk. It will require some vulnerability. It's something you won't feel comfortable doing for the first few weeks. You probably don't feel ready to do it. I get that.

But you *are* ready to spiritually bond as a couple. Now, right now, is always the best time to turn to God as a couple. The sooner you put God at the center of your relationship with these two spiritual bonding activities, the sooner He'll begin to transform your relationship.

Spiritual bonding will be hard at first. It may be uncomfortable. But don't give up. Push through the awkwardness. Praying together and talking spiritually will make a huge difference in your relationship. With God's help, you *will* break through the barriers that have kept you from experiencing deep intimacy with your spouse (and with God). Spiritual bonding will bring you closer than ever and give you the power to change the areas in your marriage that need changing.

So, listen to the doctor. Start spiritually bonding *today*.

1. Pick two of your peak couple experiences and reminisce a little. When was your last peak couple experience?
2. What kind of spiritual bonding do you do now? Why do you think you don't spiritually bond more?
3. Agree to begin spiritually bonding this week through prayer and spiritual conversations. Pray that God will help you get past your resistance and follow through.
4. Practice some spiritual bonding right now. Take just five minutes to either pray or have a spiritual conversation.

Abraham and Sarah

OUTRAGEOUS SELFISHNESS AND TRUST IN GOD

3
"Why Can't It Be about Me?"

Every time Sandy is with me at one of my marriage seminars, a wife will come up to her and gush, "Oh, you must be so blessed living with such a great husband!" To her credit, Sandy does not burst out laughing. Her typical response is: "Yes, it's quite an adventure living with Dave."

What Sandy *wants* to say to these well-meaning admirers is this: "Most of the time, Dave is a great husband. But sometimes he's a selfish jerk." And, sadly, that's the truth. I admit that I always have to fight against selfishness. As is the case with the majority of husbands, I tend to think of myself and my own needs first.

WELCOME TO MARRIAGE, SWEETHEART

In the first month of our marriage, I hit the ground running with an outrageous outburst of selfishness. Right after moving into a cramped, rat-infested apartment in Dallas, I put my beautiful blond bride to work. I was entering my second year at Dallas Theological Seminary and had to focus on my studies. Without thinking of Sandy, I dumped all the household chores on her.

When I say "all," I mean *all*: grocery shopping, cooking, dishes, laundry, cleaning, vacuuming, paying the bills. . . . My mother happily did all these jobs when I was growing up, so I figured Sandy would feel the same way. Of course, Sandy also had a full-time job outside the home.

I also added the job of *typist* to Sandy's job description. I had to crank out three or four papers a week for my professors. I was thrilled when Sandy agreed to type them for me. (This was in the days of actual typewriters, not computer word processing.) I often came down to the wire with these papers, so Sandy would stay up late typing while I went to bed. As a nasty, extra insult, she had to read my horrendous handwriting.

I honestly did not have a clue that I was mistreating my wife. I thought she wouldn't mind all these jobs. I actually believed she would be happy and fulfilled handling all these responsibilities. What a selfish numbskull I was! So, while I enjoyed a great first month of marriage, Sandy's first month of living with me was a tad short of great—as you can imagine.

After one month of doing everything, Sandy opened her mouth and said the four words that turn a husband's insides to jelly: "We need to talk." First, there was no *we*. Sandy did all the talking. Second, it wasn't a *talk*. It was a lecture.

Sandy told me I was selfish and that she needed help. She wanted to be on a *team*. She said, quite correctly, that the household chores were not *her* jobs but *our* jobs. At the end of our little meeting, I apologized for my selfishness and agreed to step up and shoulder my share of the load. For the next three years, I did the laundry, the dishes, and a portion of the cleaning. And I became my own typist again.

Over our twenty-eight years of marriage, I have been forced many times—by my precious wife—to face my selfishness. She would tell you that I've improved, but I have to watch myself very carefully. My first inclination is to think of myself and what would make my life easier.

ABRAHAM: POSTER BOY FOR SELFISH HUSBANDS

Abraham has been revered by generations of Christians (as well as Jews and Muslims) because of his tremendous faith. More than 25 percent of the book of Genesis is devoted to him. In the New Testament "Hall of Faith" in Hebrews 11, more verses are devoted to Abraham's faith than to any other hall member. Abraham is a giant in our Christian faith. So, how could he be so selfish?

Yes, despite his great faith, Abraham struggled with selfishness. As a husband, there were times he put his needs above the needs of his wife, Sarah. And not in minor, petty ways. When Abraham chose to be selfish, he did it in world-class ways. Genesis 12 showcases one example of Abraham's outrageous selfishness.

In the first part of the chapter (Genesis 12:1–9), Abraham displays remarkable faith by obeying God's command to leave his country and go to a strange land. Without knowing his destination, Abraham loads up Sarah and all their possessions and hits the road. Gutsy. Amazing. Impressive.

But then the story takes a shocking and sickening turn (Genesis 12:10–20). Because of a terrible famine, Abraham and Sarah travel to Egypt. In that day, in enemy territory, a husband could be killed for his wife. Abraham, fearing for his life, concocts a scheme to protect himself. This great man of faith asks his beautiful wife to lie and say she is his sister. Sarah was actually his half sister, but it was still a lie. She was his *full* wife!

This lie kept Abraham alive and bought him some time to figure out how to get through the famine. As Sarah's "brother," any man wanting to marry Sarah would have to negotiate a nuptial contract with him for Sarah's hand in marriage. So Abraham would be safe and be treated well. Good for him!

But what about Sarah? Frankly, he wasn't concerned for her welfare. He threw his precious wife under the bus. Or, to use an ancient term, he threw her under the camel.

"SORRY, HONEY, BUT I HAVE TO THROW YOU UNDER THE CAMEL"

Let's take a look at Abraham's selfish statements in Genesis 12:11–13 (and the comments I imagine Sarah might have made in response):

Abraham:	I know what a beautiful woman you are.
Sarah:	Uh, oh. Here comes trouble. What do you want?

Abraham:	When the Egyptians see you, they will say, "This is his wife."
Sarah:	Of course, because I am your wife. So?
Abraham:	Then they will kill me but will let you live.
Sarah:	Number one, you don't know for sure they will kill you. Number two, aren't you willing to die to protect me and my honor? Number three, don't you believe God will protect you? He just gave you a wonderful promise that He will make you into a great nation. In order to fulfill that promise, He will have to keep you alive!
Abraham:	Say you are my sister. . . .
Sarah:	You don't even have the guts to do your own lying! You're going to make me lie for you!
Abraham:	. . .so that I will be treated well for your sake and my life will be spared because of you.
Sarah:	Well, by all means, let's make sure you will be treated well! Saving your life is our top priority! It's all about you, isn't it, Abraham? What about me? You are leaving me vulnerable and unprotected! I'm supposed to become another man's wife to keep you safe?

Of course, the Bible has no record of what Sarah said in response to Abraham's selfish statements. But even though she went along with Abraham's scheme, I like to imagine that she assertively stood up for herself and the truth.

Predictably, Abraham's plan was a disaster. At least for Sarah. The most powerful man in Egypt, the Pharaoh himself, took Sarah as his wife and placed her in his harem. Who knows what indignities, sexual or otherwise, she had to suffer? Abraham, however, was living the high life. Pharaoh gave him sheep, cattle, donkeys, servants, and camels. For Abraham, it was like winning the lottery.

God soon intervened, as He did again when Abraham engaged in this abominable behavior a second time (Genesis 20), by sending diseases on Pharaoh and his family. When Pharaoh discovered Abraham's lie, he expelled him from his kingdom and gave Sarah back to him, along with some scathing words. So, Sarah was rescued, but Abraham's selfishness must have damaged her and their marriage. Her respect, love, and trust in him must have plummeted. How could it not?

"I'VE GOT TO SAVE MYSELF!"

Many husbands, myself included, will act selfishly to protect themselves from painful and unpleasant responsibilities. We selfishly avoid chores around the home. We selfishly refuse to deal with conflict with our wives. We selfishly decide not to back our wives in the discipline of the children. We selfishly side with our biological children if we are in a blended family. We selfishly choose not to stand up to our parents when our wives are in conflict with them. We selfishly continue to work long hours at our jobs. We selfishly spend too much time on our leisure activities. And some husbands will break their wives' hearts by being unfaithful.

Husband, be honest with me and with your wife. Admit you're guilty of some of these selfish actions. Most husbands struggle with selfishness. Husbands have a genetic predisposition to protect themselves at the expense of their wives. The truth is, selfish actions do not satisfy. Selfish actions do great damage to a marriage.

STAND UP, STEP UP, AND MAN UP

Your selfishness is deeply wounding your precious wife. It's time—right now—to begin thinking of her and her needs *first*. After your relationship and fellowship with the Lord, your relationship and fellowship with your wife is to be your number one priority. In every situation, no matter how potentially awkward or difficult, your job is to protect her and do what is best for her. When you value her as God values her (Ephesians 5:25, 28, 31) and put her immediately after God in importance in your life, the love and respect you receive from her will far outweigh the pain you experience by meeting her needs.

Ask your wife to name the areas where you have been selfish. Ask her how you can specifically change in those areas. Give her permission to tell you when you're being selfish. Believe her when she calls you on it. Don't insult her by being defensive. If she says you're being selfish, you're being selfish, because what's important to you is how she *feels*.

Do not put your career above your wife. Work hard, but don't work an excessive number of hours. Make time for her each week. Don't spend too much time on your leisure activities. You're not a single man anymore. Make sure your wife's and children's needs for time and attention are met before you engage in your own fun activities.

Do your fair share of the chores around the home. When you finish your regular chores, ask her what else needs to be done. When there is a conflict between you and her, face it directly and talk it through with her. When your wife is in a conflict with another person (a child or stepchild, your parents or hers, another family member, a friend, a tradesperson), be on her side. Do not be critical of her in front of anyone. It's okay to disagree in private, but in public or when the children are present, be completely supportive of her. If necessary, intervene for her in a dispute.

THE POWER OF A WOMAN'S EMOTIONS

Every husband knows that nuclear energy is not the most

powerful force on earth. It's not even a close second. The most powerful and awesome force on earth is a woman's emotions. Nothing can match it in sheer intensity and shocking impact. I truly believe that one twenty-minute outburst from a woman could power a small town for three days.

Let me give you an example. One morning, not too long ago, Sandy was in a strange mood. She seemed cold and reserved and looked at me with suspicion. I went to kiss her, as I always do in the morning, and she gave me her cheek. Not a good sign. I said, "Honey, what's wrong?"

"I dreamed about you last night, and I'm very upset about it."

"What? Tell me about it."

"In my dream, we had a terrible argument, and you said awful things to me. You were so cold and harsh and uncaring."

"But it was a *dream*. It didn't really happen. I was asleep the entire time. So were you!"

"I know, but I just can't shake my feelings of anger, hurt, and disgust. You treated me so badly."

"But it was just a dream."

"After you chewed me out, you laughed and left to go to work. I was stunned. I mean, I thought I knew you! I thought you'd never treat me that way!"

"I *wouldn't* treat you that way! I love you. We have our conflicts, but I wouldn't verbally abuse you. Remember, this was a dream."

Even though Sandy knew it was a dream, her emotional response was so intense that she *felt* as if the nasty argument had actually happened. Her emotions—temporarily—overrode her rational thinking. After several hours, her emotional reaction subsided, and I was back in her good graces.

A woman tends to be driven by her emotions. It's common for her emotions to dictate a course of action. When a woman feels strongly about something, she's convinced she's right. That, of course, means the man is wrong. This kind of emotional reasoning can easily lead to incorrect, selfish decisions. It's certainly not intentional or malicious. It just tends to happen.

Here's the chain of emotional reasoning that many wives experience:

1. I feel very intensely about something.
2. Because I feel so strongly about it, my position must be right.
3. My emotions override what God says and my husband thinks.
4. I will do whatever it takes to get what I want.

SARAH WAS SELFISH TOO

As we've seen, Abraham was selfish. Big-time selfish. He protected himself at Sarah's expense. But he wasn't the only selfish one in the marriage. Sarah was just as selfish in her own way. She made the mistake that wives have made for centuries: she allowed her emotions to lead to self-serving, sinful behavior.

In Genesis 16:1–6, we read that Sarah's powerful emotions about having a baby led her to make a series of very poor decisions. God had promised Abraham and Sarah a natural child, but Sarah ran out of patience waiting to get pregnant. She let her emotions—frustration, deep disappointment, and anger at God—drive her to make poor decision number one: she demanded that Abraham sleep with her maidservant, Hagar.

When Hagar got pregnant, she despised Sarah. This upset Sarah so much that she made poor decision number two: she blamed Abraham for Hagar's treatment of her. Talk about strong emotions overriding reason! It was Sarah's idea for Abraham to have a child by Hagar, a child that Sarah would take as her own. It's true that Abraham should have refused to do this, but Sarah should have accepted at least half the blame for coming up with this baby-making scheme.

Sarah's rage, humiliation, and insecurity motivated her to make poor decision number three: she seriously mistreated Hagar. Hagar felt so abused that she ran away.

"I Want a Baby. . .Now!"

Here are Sarah's selfish statements in Genesis 16:2–5, with the comments I imagine Abraham might have—and *should* have—made in response:

Sarah:	The Lord has kept me from having children.
Abraham:	Honey, I know you desperately want a child. I do too. It's okay to be angry at God for not coming through yet. But God promised to give us a baby. He will deliver in His timing.
Sarah:	Go, sleep with my maidservant; perhaps I can build a family through her.
Abraham:	First, that sounds like a command and not a request. Also, this approach may be culturally acceptable, but I don't want to sleep with another woman. I won't do it, because it will hurt you, me, and Hagar. This is your way, not God's way. Take some time to think and pray about it.

Later, after Hagar becomes pregnant:

Sarah:	You are responsible for the wrong I am suffering. I put my servant in your arms, and now that she knows she is pregnant, she despises me.
Abraham:	I'm responsible? You've got to be kidding! This was your idea, not mine! I shouldn't have gone along with it, that's true; but you need to take responsibility too. She wouldn't

be despising you if you hadn't put her in my arms. You ought to be angry not at Hagar and me, but at yourself!

If only Abraham had given these types of rational, assertive responses, things would have turned out differently. What Abraham did instead was wilt in the face of Sarah's intense emotions. He passively agreed to Sarah's order to sleep with Hagar, maybe as a way to make up for the "say you are my sister" fiasco. Sarah's plan was a disaster that caused heartbreak for her, for Hagar, and for Abraham.

Once again, God saved Sarah and Abraham from themselves. He intervened to protect Hagar and her son. Despite Sarah's emotionally driven, disobedient-to-God choices, God kept His promise and gave her and Abraham a son—*the* son—to continue the line of God's people. But Sarah's actions took a toll on her marriage, and many have suffered greatly through the ages because of her decision.

"I'm Right, So Let's Do It My Way"

Many wives, my Sandy included, often make the mistake of allowing their emotions to control their behavior. I believe this is because women filter everything through a screen of emotions; they *feel*, and they feel *deeply*. Wife, when you feel strongly about an issue, you believe you're right. You naturally stay focused on your own position and have trouble seeing your husband's side of things. You convince yourself that your position is the only correct one.

When you believe you are right and your husband is wrong, there is zero chance to successfully resolve the conflict. The key to working through marital conflicts is respecting and understanding your spouse's position. If you stay locked into your point of view, there can be only one of two outcomes. And both are bad. One, you and your husband remain stuck in a standoff and never figure out a plan of action. Or two, you get your way, and your marriage suffers as a result.

If you get your way too much of the time, you'll lose respect for your husband as a man and as a leader. You'll be less and less interested in his opinion, because what he thinks and feels doesn't matter to you. Also, he will lose all kinds of respect and love for you. He'll feel increasingly weak and unnecessary in the relationship. He'll resent you and pull away from you.

Your tendency to believe you're right—based on your emotions—is particularly dangerous when you and your husband are facing life's big decisions:

- having a baby
- parenting a child
- choosing a church
- changing jobs
- moving
- buying big-ticket items (such as a home, car, major appliance) or remodeling
- handling financial issues, such as budget planning, choosing investments
- dealing with in-laws and other family members

If you shut your husband out of these large-impact decisions, you will do serious, lasting damage to your marriage. I've seen many marriages destroyed because the wife had to have her way in these areas.

"Am I in the Right if My Husband Is Sinning?"
The one time you are absolutely, 100 percent right in taking a firm stand opposing your husband's view is when your husband is sinning. If he's physically violent with you or the kids. If he's engaging in adultery. If he's watching pornography. If he's flirting with other women. If he's drinking too much. If he's abusing illegal or prescription drugs. If he's gambling. If he's verbally abusive. If he's a workaholic. If he's involved in unethical or illegal business deals.

When your husband chooses to sin, your emotions about his behavior need to be expressed fully and firmly. And directly to him in person. Your position that he is out of God's will and way out of line is correct. You are totally right and he is totally wrong.

Don't let anyone—especially him—convince you that you are emotionally overreacting, being a nag, or acting in a controlling way. That's baloney. It's bad advice and it's not biblical. Keep expressing your emotions with him and assertively confront his sinful behavior.

LEARN TO LISTEN AND RESPECT YOUR HUSBAND'S POINT OF VIEW

You're an emotional person. That's fine. That's healthy. That's how God made you. But God did not make you right about everything. A strong emotional response means you really care about the situation. It does not mean you are right. It does not mean you are entitled to get what you want.

Your point of view is exactly that: *your point of view*. It is important that you express your emotions and your point of view to your husband. It is equally important that you allow your husband to express his emotions and his point of view. And not merely *allow* it. Your job is to listen to him and fully respect what he has to say. His position is just as valid as yours.

In every conflict, there are two truths. There is your truth, and there is your husband's truth. Take it slow, and—one at a time—get these two truths out on the table. Take the time to listen, reflect, process, and understand each other's truths. Give your emotions time to settle down. Work hard to see the issue from each other's vantage point.

If your emotions escalate and make it difficult to understand your husband's position, call for a time-out. Get some space to think it through and pray. Then go to your husband and ask him to continue the discussion.

Make prayer a part of the decision-making process. Pray together that God will help you understand each other's positions and reach the right decision. In the big decisions of life, search the Bible for God's direction and seek out godly, knowledgeable advisers for counsel. (More on this in the next chapter.)

By involving God and truly respecting each other's emotions and opinions, you will be able to resolve every conflict and make good, godly decisions.

Outrageous Interaction

1. Husband, ask your wife to list your top three selfish areas.
2. Husband, ask your wife how you can specifically change in these areas in order to protect her and put her welfare first.
3. Wife, ask your husband to list three times when he has noticed your emotions overriding your ability to consider his point of view.
4. Wife, agree to respect your husband's point of view, and add more discussion and prayer to the decision-making process.

4
"What Does God Want Us to Do?"

When a husband has an important decision to make, he wants as much input as possible from others. He will immediately contact his closest family members and friends and talk with each of them about the decision. Some of these conversations will be lengthy, because he tends to go over and over the same details. He'll talk to several of these key support persons more than once in an attempt to get their opinions on every facet of the looming decision.

All right, I can't keep going on like this. You realize I'm kidding, right? A husband would never take this approach. This is how a wife operates when she faces a decision.

A husband immediately goes into solitary mode when he has a critical decision to make. At most, he'll talk to one or two men about it. Maybe his dad and a friend. It's his decision, and he'll make the best decision he can on his own. Internally, he thinks about all angles of the decision. It's a logical, methodical, and mostly secret process.

He certainly considers his wife and how she'll be affected by the decision, but he does not typically involve her in the process. Often, she has no idea he's making a decision. When he completes his one-man journey, he will inform his wife of his conclusions. He sincerely believes his decision is the best one for all concerned. He is surprised by his wife's negative reaction to being left out of the decision-making loop.

"By the Way, I've Chosen a New Career"
It was near the end of my last year at Dallas Theological Seminary. My career path was set in stone. Sandy and I were in agreement that I was going to be a psychologist. After Dallas, we'd move to Portland, Oregon, where I'd enter a doctoral program at Western Seminary. I had already been accepted at Western. What could go wrong?

Suddenly, out of nowhere, I wasn't sure about becoming a psychologist. I got the idea that I should be a youth pastor instead. I'd always loved kids and had worked at two Christian summer camps during my college years. For three weeks, I agonized over this decision. I spoke to my dad and to my favorite seminary professor. Foolishly, I didn't say one word to Sandy.

After three weeks, I made up my mind and informed Sandy that I wanted to become a youth pastor. Her first reaction was anger and hurt because I had completely cut her out of the process. She said to me, "Dave, how could you not include me in this big decision? I'm your wife! We're supposed to be on the same team and share everything. If you really want to be a youth pastor, I'll support you. But we need to talk about decisions like this."

She was 100 percent correct. I had told her nothing, because I didn't want her to see my insecurity and fear about the future. But, as my wife, she had every right to know my feelings and thoughts about my career. I apologized for wounding her and committed to include her in future decisions.

Then Sandy hit me with her second reaction: "A youth pastor? Are you nuts? I think you'd be a much better psychologist." It turned out she was right about that too. I dropped the youth pastor idea soon after our talk, and we got back on the psychology track.

"I've Taken a Poll, and Emily Should Sing"

When our first child, Emily, was five years old, she loved to sing and was in the children's choir at our church. The choir director asked us if Emily could sing a solo during a Sunday morning worship service. Sandy and I had a discussion about it. I thought Emily was too young to sing by herself in front of the whole church. Sandy was pretty sure Emily could pull it off and that the experience would boost her self-esteem and confidence.

Sandy immediately went into consensus mode as she wrestled with the situation. As women often do, she involved a host of other persons in her decision-making process. She talked about Emily's potential solo with her mother. My mother. The choir director. A neighbor lady. And three or four of her close female friends.

After each of these conversations, Sandy came to me and reported what each person said. She was doing what most wives do to make a decision: getting input from multiple sources in order to build a consensus. If the majority of these persons believed Emily should sing, she'd feel much better about that choice.

As I watched Sandy talk to all these people, I thought to myself, *What a waste of time! Life is too short to gather all these votes. And what do these people know about it, anyway? We can make this decision ourselves. Why don't we just hire a pollster and find out what all of America thinks about Emily's singing a solo?* (Fortunately, I was too smart to say these things to Sandy.)

I liked the fact that I was in the decision-making loop, but I felt insulted because it appeared that my opinion was no more important than anyone else's. Sandy was talking to me about the decision, and I had a vote, but I could easily be outvoted by the peanut gallery—I mean, this important group of family and friends. Getting a majority vote was clearly more valuable to Sandy than my input.

Do you know what happened? I was outvoted. Big surprise, huh? Most of the voters thought we should let Emily sing the solo. Reluctantly, I agreed, and Emily pulled it off beautifully, so letting her sing may have been the right decision. But I was unsettled by the way we made the decision. I didn't like the fact that the opinions of others carried so much weight.

I told Sandy, "I don't appreciate being merely one more opinion among many. I don't have a problem with your talking over the situation with trusted supporters, but I want *my* opinion to be the most important and influential." Sandy heard me out and agreed to elevate my point of view on decisions to the number one slot. (Actually, the number two slot, as I'll explain shortly.)

Work as a Team, and Do It God's Way

There is one major flaw in the way most husbands and wives go about making important decisions. This fundamental, and fatal, flaw is that they both depend on the wrong source for direction. The husband relies primarily on *himself*, while the wife relies primarily on her *circle of supporters*.

When you choose to rely on human reasoning alone to make a decision, you're asking for trouble. Human intelligence and insight are the cause of many poor decisions. The human mind is subjective, limited, often distorted, and self-serving.

The key to effective decision-making is for the husband and wife, working as a team, to look to *God* for guidance. God knows everything. He knows the right decision in every situation. What's more, God loves you and your marriage, and He wants to help you make excellent decisions that are good for your relationship and honoring to Him.

Abraham and Sarah certainly made some very bad decisions. Horrifically bad decisions. We saw that in the last chapter. But they also made some great decisions. When Abraham and Sarah chose to follow God's direction, the results were spectacular: their faith in God grew stronger, God blessed them, and their marriage was strengthened.

The Outrageous Faith of Abraham and Sarah

In the span of eleven chapters (Genesis 12–22), Abraham and Sarah faced four major decisions. Huge, extremely difficult, and life-changing decisions. In each case, they showed outrageous faith in God by doing what *He* wanted them to do.

Even though the biblical account describes only what Abraham did, I am convinced that Sarah was intimately involved in each decision.

Why do I believe this? Two reasons.

First, Sarah was a very feisty and independent-minded woman, who had no trouble speaking her mind to Abraham. We see this saucy, I-will-speak-my-mind attitude in Genesis 16, when Sarah orders Abraham to sleep with Hagar. Then, when that action backfires on her, she has the nerve to blame Abraham. Sarah was one spunky gal!

In Genesis 21, Sarah again assertively speaks her mind to Abraham. She's angry at Hagar's son, Ishmael, and demands that Abraham "drive out this maid and her son" (Genesis 21:10). These are not the words of a passive, mousy woman. Sarah was a headstrong, blunt-talking wife, who had a strong voice in her marriage. Whether he wanted to or not, Abraham always knew what Sarah thought and felt.

My second reason for suspecting that Sarah was involved in these critical decisions with Abraham is found in 1 Peter 3:5–6. In this passage, Sarah is held up as an example of submissiveness:

> *For in this way in former times the holy women also, who hoped in God, used to adorn themselves, being submissive to their own husbands; just as Sarah obeyed Abraham, calling him lord, and you have become her children if you do what is right without being frightened by any fear.*

Sarah is singled out as a shining example of how to be submissive to your husband. Why praise her for being submissive if she knew nothing about these major decisions? You certainly can't "obey" your husband if you don't have a clue about what he plans to do. I believe Sarah was a key player on the team, voicing her point of view and working closely with Abraham as he was doing what God wanted him to do.

DECISION NUMBER ONE: "LET'S LEAVE OUR HOME AND GO TO A STRANGE LAND"

When we first meet Abraham, he is a comfortable, wealthy, middle-aged man, who has *zero* relationship with God. Out of nowhere, God suddenly tells him to leave everything—his home, his father, his family—and travel to a strange country. God promises to bless him richly. But for all Abraham knew, these were just words. The blessings hadn't happened yet. Demonstrating remarkable faith in God, Abraham gathers up Sarah and all their possessions and servants and sets out for the land of Canaan.

God protected the couple on their journey and eventually did all He had promised them. Abraham and Sarah's outrageous faith was generously rewarded. Outrageous faith always is.

Decision Number Two: "Lot, Take the Best Land"

Abraham and his nephew, Lot, were traveling together. The problem was the land could not sustain their substantial households and possessions. They needed to separate. Abraham graciously allowed Lot to choose where he would settle. Lot selfishly chose the best part: the lush, well-watered plain of the Jordan.

God had already promised Abraham all of this land. He had every right to choose the best part. Why didn't he? Because of his faith in God. Abraham knew that God would take care of him, no matter which plot of land Lot chose.

After Abraham let Lot choose, God confirmed Abraham's act of faith by telling him that He would give him and his descendants forever all the land he could see (Genesis 13:14–15). Abraham and Sarah's outrageous faith was generously rewarded. Outrageous faith always is.

Decision Number Three: "I'm Going to Rescue Lot from the Four Kings"

Lot, who had a knack for getting himself into trouble, was captured by four marauding kings, the baddest guys around, who were undefeated in a series of wars and had seized a huge expanse of land. Who would be crazy enough to take on these kings? Abraham never flinched as he decided to rescue Lot from these powerful monarchs. Abraham knew that God would be on his side in the battle. Sure enough, God gave Abraham a great victory.

After Abraham's stunning military success, God confirmed his faithful actions by blessing him through a king and priest named Melchizedek (Genesis 14:18–20), and by reaffirming the promises He had made earlier (Genesis 15:1–7). Abraham and Sarah's outrageous faith was generously rewarded. Outrageous faith always is.

DECISION NUMBER FOUR: "I WILL SACRIFICE MY SON"

This fourth decision was, by far, the most difficult. The word *difficult* doesn't even begin to describe it. God instructed Abraham to take his only son, Isaac, and kill him as a burnt offering. How could God ask such a thing of Abraham? God had promised Abraham and Sarah that, through Isaac, He would bless them with descendants who would number "as the dust of the earth...too many to count." With Isaac dead, those promises would also be dead.

In a display of faith that defies explanation, Abraham obeyed God and came within a whisker of killing Isaac. God wanted to try Abraham's faith, and Abraham passed the test. So, God spared Isaac and repeated to Abraham the promises He had made to him.

Once again, Abraham and Sarah showed outrageous faith, and it was generously rewarded. Outrageous faith always is.

IF IT WORKED FOR ABRAHAM AND SARAH, IT WILL WORK FOR YOU AND YOUR SPOUSE

In each of these four decisions, Abraham and Sarah did it God's way. Their focus was not on what *they each* wanted to do. Their focus was on listening to God and obeying His directions. Every time Abraham and Sarah followed God's leading, they were abundantly blessed. God's way is always the right way.

When we as couples do what God wants us to do, we get a "double whammy" of blessing. Because God's way is always correct, the first whammy is that our decisions will be correct and life will work out better. Because God is pleased when we obey Him (John 15:10, 14), the second whammy is that He will bless us in additional ways! Just as God showered

Abraham and Sarah with blessings after they obeyed Him, He will shower us with blessings after we obey Him. That's a sweet deal!

God spoke clearly to Abraham and Sarah. God speaks just as clearly to us today, though He uses different methods. I believe God spoke audibly to Abraham and Sarah. It's unlikely that He will speak to you and me audibly today. But, in a variety of ways, He will reveal to us what He wants us to do:

- through *scripture* (Abraham and Sarah did not have the immense advantage and blessing that we have of a written Word from God.)
- through *prayer*
- through the *Holy Spirit* guiding our decisions (Abraham and Sarah did not have the indwelling Holy Spirit.)
- through *godly counsel*
- through *God-ordained circumstances*

God will allow us to make decisions without Him. He will not stop us from making choices based on our selfish desires. We have seen what happened to Abraham and Sarah when they excluded God from decisions and did what they each wanted to do. Absolute disaster and tremendous, ongoing pain.

God desires to lead you and your spouse as a couple to make decisions that will glorify Him and bring you closer in your relationship. The secret to good marital decisions is to keep your focus on God and what He wants you to do. Here's how:

A FIVE-STEP, GOD-CENTERED DECISION-MAKING PROCESS

Sandy and I have developed a five-step process that helps us make God-directed decisions. I'm not saying we follow this process for all our decisions. When we fail to follow these five steps, we suffer the consequences (and, as the leader, I take responsibility for those times). But when we follow these five steps, we reap the rewards.

STEP ONE: FIRST MEETING

Start by sitting down with your spouse to have an initial discussion about the decision you're facing. This meeting ought to begin with prayer. Hold hands and take turns praying that God will guide you in the process and show you the course of action He wants you to take.

After praying, share with each other your thoughts and feelings about the decision. When one of you is speaking, the other person becomes the *Listener*. The Listener's job is *not* to interject his or her opinion. The Listener's job is to *communicate understanding* of the *Speaker's* position by reflecting back the Speaker's opinions and emotions. The Listener doesn't have to agree: The point is to *actively build understanding* of the Speaker's point of view. The Listener does not share his or her opinion, or add anything original to the conversation, when the Speaker is speaking.

When the Speaker says that he or she feels understood, take a brief break. Get a drink, go to the bathroom, or feed the dog. After a few minutes, continue the discussion with the roles reversed. Now the original Listener becomes the Speaker and shares honestly his or her thoughts and feelings about the decision. The new Listener works to *communicate understanding* of the Speaker's position.

In this initial meeting, both husband and wife are trying to discover what God wants you *as a couple* to do. Of course, you share your own opinions and feelings and preferences. That's normal and healthy. But you keep your mind on what God's principles, commands, and preferences might be.

End this meeting with another brief prayer, asking God to reveal His direction to you as the process continues.

STEP TWO: JUST YOU AND GOD

In this step, you each agree to spend private time with God, seeking His will for the looming decision. This you-and-God time could be several days to a week in length. You don't talk to anyone else during this step. You think about the decision from all angles and listen to God through prayer and reading the Bible.

STEP THREE: LET'S TALK

Now it's time to get together again as a couple and share what you learned during your time of seeking God's will. One at a time, communicate what God has revealed through your prayer and Bible reading. Sometimes God will reveal His direction to both spouses during the "just you and God" step. Obviously, if God does it this way, the decision is apparent and the process is over.

Sometimes God will choose to reveal His direction to only one spouse. I don't know why He would do this, but God gets to do it His way. If one spouse believes that God has made His will clear, both spouses need to discuss it and pray about it. This may take twenty minutes or several days.

If the other spouse comes to believe that the decision is God's will, then the process is over. You have your decision. If not, go on to step four.

STEP FOUR: SEEK GODLY COUNSEL

You're looking for God's plan of action, and He has chosen not to uncover it—yet. So you seek godly counsel from people you know well and trust completely.

Sometimes God chooses to speak through godly individuals, such as your pastor, a Christian counselor, a family member, or a close friend.

If possible, talk to these counselors together. If you must speak to someone alone, fully inform your spouse about the conversation as soon as you can. Even if these godly individuals are not able to provide God's clear answer, their wisdom and insights are invaluable.

STEP FIVE: THE HUSBAND MAKES THE CALL

Ninety-five percent of the time, God will reveal His answer to one or both of you in the first four steps. When He doesn't, the husband will have to make the decision, because the Bible teaches that the husband is the leader in the marriage and family and is responsible before God for his marriage and children (Ephesians 5:22–24; 6:4). If it comes to this, the husband must make the decision carefully and prayerfully and only after completing the first four steps. Only when he can say to his spouse, "I understand your feelings and your perspective, and I respect them. I have gone to God, and I believe He is telling us to do the following." The wife's role is to submit to his decision and support it. Unless it is a violation of God's principles in scripture, a sinful choice, the wife must support it.

IT'S GOD'S WAY OR THE HIGHWAY

Important decisions are not about what you, as individuals or as a couple, want. They are about what God wants. In my experience, both personal and professional, making decisions with this five-step process will accomplish the following:

- lead to the right decisions so life will work out better

- make you closer and more intimate as a couple
- deepen your individual spiritual lives
- create an outrageous faith as a couple
- produce God's blessings in many areas of your lives

Outrageous Interaction

1. Husband, describe a time when, facing an important decision, you used the solitary approach (i.e., told your wife nothing and simply informed her of what you had decided). Ask your wife how that made her feel.
2. Wife, describe a time when, facing an important decision, you used the consensus approach (i.e., talked to your circle of supporters and took a vote). Ask your husband how that made him feel.
3. Think of a time when you were single, when God clearly guided you to make a certain decision. How did God make it clear?
4. Talk about a decision you made as a couple by following God's direction. How did God speak to you? What was the result of the decision? Agree to work as a team to follow God's guidance in every key decision. Next time you face such a decision, practice the five-step process outlined in this chapter.

Jacob, Leah, and Rachel

OUTRAGEOUS PASSIVITY, DISRESPECT, AND COMMITMENT

5
The Wimp and the Witch

A couple whom I'll call Bob and Betty came to me for marriage counseling. At our first session, after getting some information about them as individuals, I asked each one to tell me about the major problem in their marriage. Twenty minutes later, I knew I was facing one of the most common, and most damaging, marital problems, which I affectionately call "The Wimp and the Witch."

Betty: Dr. Clarke, I am sick and tired of having to carry the entire load of this marriage and family! Bob works hard at his job, but when he's home, he's totally checked out. I make all the decisions concerning the kids and the home. I help the kids with their homework, I talk with their teachers, I pack their lunches and wash their clothes, and I discipline them. All he does is play with the kids. I feel like he's just another one of the kids!

Even though I work outside the home, I still do most of the chores. Also, Bob won't handle anything that makes him uncomfortable. He won't deal with family members, salespeople, or repair persons. He reminds me of a scared little boy. He often escapes by watching television, using the computer, working in the yard, or dinking around in the garage.

He won't take me out on dates. He won't spend time talking with me. He just avoids me! I ask him to do things and he'll agree but then doesn't follow through. That makes him a liar.

When it comes to big decisions, such as making investments or buying big-ticket items, Bob shuts me out of the process. He'll make the decision and then inform me. Would somebody please tell Bob that I want to be on the same team with him? I want to do things together. I want him to lead this family. I can't tell you how utterly frustrated, exhausted, and unhappy I am!

Bob: Dave, I just can't please Betty. No matter what I do, it's never good enough. I guess I got tired of trying, because nothing I've done has ever made her happy. I work hard at my job, and when I get home, I'm tired. I want a break from making decisions and facing difficult issues. I want some peace and quiet. Is that a crime?

She's always asking me to do things around the home. I don't mind doing some things, but when I do a chore, it's never fast enough or the way she wants it done. So what's the point of doing anything for her? All I hear is criticism and disappointment. A little encouragement would go a long way. So, yeah, I do less around the home than I should, and I stay at work longer. At least at work I feel appreciated and get some praise.

When Betty says, "We need to talk," I know she's mad about something and it's going to be a fight. I can't stand conflict with her because I get raked over the coals and she doesn't want to hear my side of the story. Plus, she wants an immediate answer from me, and I don't know what to say. I can't think on my feet as quickly as she can.

I've let her do what she wants with the kids and the home. I thought that would make her happy. I want some respect. I want her to be warm and loving. I want to be with her physically, but she rejects my advances most of the time. I do avoid her because she makes me feel like a loser and a failure.

SOME STRAIGHT TALK

Well, you've figured out by now that Bob is the Wimp and Betty is the Witch. The Wimp is the passive husband who won't provide the leadership his wife longs for and needs and that his family needs. The Witch is the disrespectful wife who won't submit to her husband. It is not one spouse's fault. It is the fault of both spouses, because they both play their parts in the pattern. It is a nasty pattern that, if not stopped, will kill all intimacy in a marriage. And once intimacy is dead, the marriage is in real trouble.

When I see a couple with this passive husband/disrespectful wife pattern, I begin the change process with some straight talk to each spouse. I sit down privately with each one and lower the boom of truth.

Bob

"Bob, the last thing you want is a controlling nag of a wife who is critical and cold most of the time. But that's what you have, isn't it? And do you know whose fault it is? It's *your* fault, Bob, because you're acting like a wimp. You're passive at home and force Betty to be the leader. When conflict occurs with Betty, you run away like a ten-year-old boy. If you wanted peace and quiet and no conflict, why did you get married?

"You have put her in charge of the home and the kids. So that's why she's telling you what to do. You don't like being controlled, do you? You get angry and defensive and fight back by avoiding her and not doing your assigned tasks in a timely manner. Your choice to be passive has made you the little boy and Betty your mother.

"A wife cannot respect a husband who refuses to lead. The path to a warm, soft, and affectionate wife is to 'man up' and start leading her in the relationship and in the family. I know you don't know how to be a leader. I'm going to teach you how."

Betty

"Betty, I know you are extremely frustrated, angry, and wounded because Bob is so passive at home. You're the leader by default and have to make sure everything gets done. Bob has dumped the whole load of responsibility on you, and you have a right to be very upset about that.

"But you don't have a right to mistreat him, and that's what you're doing. You're acting like a witch. You are way too critical of Bob. No matter what he does, it's not good enough. You demean him. You belittle him, even in front of the kids. You have become a disrespectful wife.

"It is no wonder why Bob works longer hours at his job, tries to avoid you, and does fewer and fewer chores. It's his way of fighting back and preserving his feelings of manhood. And no husband wants to romantically pursue a wife who is cold and mean.

"Betty, your negative attitude and controlling behavior will never motivate Bob to change. He clearly needs to learn how to lead you, and we'll work on that. But you have to learn how to respectfully submit to his leadership, thereby cultivating leadership in him. I'm going to teach you how."

THE ORIGINAL WIMP AND WITCHES

Jacob, the Old Testament patriarch and a man richly blessed by God, was a wimp. His wives, Leah and Rachel, were witches. There, I said it. Jacob was pathetically passive, and Leah and Rachel were incredibly disrespectful and controlling. Let's take a look at the originators of the Wimp and the Witch marital pattern. We can learn a great deal from their mistakes.

THE OLD TESTAMENT WORKAHOLIC

Jacob was a very driven, type A workaholic. As many men tend to do, he focused obsessively on his career. He connived with his mother, Rebekah, to get his father Isaac's blessing (Genesis 27:1–40). He built a significant amount of wealth through hard work and deception (Genesis 30:25–43).

Jacob desperately wanted to be a success, and he achieved that goal in terms of career advancement and possessions. But, as it happens with nearly every workaholic, his marriage and his family life suffered great damage along the way to his material success. Jacob was as passive at home as he was aggressive and in control in the workplace.

"I DON'T LOVE YOU"

Get ready to read some of the saddest words in the book of Genesis:

> *So Jacob went in to Rachel also, and indeed he loved Rachel more than Leah.*
>
> GENESIS 29:30

> *Now the LORD saw that Leah was unloved, and He opened her womb.*
>
> GENESIS 29:31

Isn't that heartbreaking? For years, Leah tried to get Jacob to love her. Every time she gave birth to a son, she hoped and prayed Jacob would be moved to love her. Tragically, he never did. In fact, Jacob never even attempted to love Leah. Though he had been tricked into marrying her (Genesis 29:1–29), he certainly could have worked at building the relationship. But he never did. He could have asked God to give him love for Leah, but nowhere in the recorded account does it say that he did.

Jacob's passivity was expressed, in part, by his lack of love for Leah. He ignored her. He did not give her loving attention. He did not pursue her conversationally or romantically. This was cruel and unusual punishment, and Leah suffered greatly.

Actually, this kind of behavior by a husband is not so unusual. Many husbands do what Jacob did. They choose to passively ignore their wives and withhold love from them.

Actively *loving* your wife (Ephesians 5:25, 28, 33; Colossians 3:19; 1 Peter 3:7) is an essential element in leadership. *Expressing* your love for her daily gives her and your children security, strengthens your love for her, increases her love for you, and teaches the children valuable lessons about marital love. Love is something you *do*.

THE ULTIMATE BABY-MAKING COMPETITION

Genesis 30:1–24 describes a vicious, pull-no-punches competition between Leah and Rachel. Jacob's two wives, who hated each other's guts, battled to see who could have the most babies. As they fought for baby-making supremacy, the two divas disrespected Jacob and completely controlled him. Jacob the wimp did nothing to stop the feud and meekly allowed his two wives to dominate him.

In Genesis 30:1–8, Rachel begins the fertility contest with these "sweet" words: "Give me children, or I'll die!" Not exactly a loving discussion about family planning. Jacob got angry and talked tough to Rachel, but he quickly caved in to her demands. Rachel ordered Jacob to sleep with her maidservant,

Bilhah. Like a good little husband, Jacob did, and two sons were born.

As recorded in Genesis 30:9–13, Leah struck back at Rachel in the war of baby making. Leah, using Rachel's playbook, had Jacob sleep with her maidservant, Zilpah. (Boy, the maidservants in Jacob's home were sure kept busy!) Zilpah gave birth to two sons. Leah was thrilled: "Happy am I! For women will call me happy" (Genesis 30:13). Jacob probably wasn't quite as happy. But it was his own foolish fault for not standing up to Leah's sexual orders.

Rachel and Leah continued their competition by making a crazy deal (Genesis 30:14–16). Their agreement brought their disrespect for Jacob to a whole new level. In return for some mandrake plants, which were considered aphrodisiacs in that day, Rachel "allowed" Leah to have sex with Jacob. The nerve of Rachel! It wasn't her place to decide that Jacob should sleep with Leah! Who made Rachel queen? What a witch!

But Rachel wasn't the only witch in this bizarre scenario. When Jacob came home from work, Leah greeted him with these lovely words: "You must come in to me, for I have surely hired you" (Genesis 30:16). First of all, a wife has no right to order her husband to have sex with her. Second, it was a slap in Jacob's face to tell him that she hired his sexual services. She treated Jacob like a gigolo!

Jacob's response to Leah *should* have been: "What, are you nuts? Please tell me you're kidding! Who is the head of this household? Who put you and Rachel in charge? Oh, yeah, *I* did. But that's over now. I will not be your on-demand sex slave. I'm sick and tired of this ridiculous contest between you and Rachel. I'm not sleeping with either of you or any maidservants until you both grow up and learn to get along. There are going to be some changes around here, starting today."

Of course, Jacob didn't respond in this assertive, leader-like way. Genesis 30:16 records his response to Leah's demand: "So he lay with her that night." What a pathetic wimp! He was a puppet on a string held by these two control freaks! He was willing to do anything to avoid conflict and keep the peace.

Amazingly, God continued to bless Jacob and Leah and Rachel despite their sinful, dysfunctional behavior. But their home wasn't happy. Or content. Or peaceful. Or intimate. It was a disaster area filled with strife and bitterness and outrageously sinful behavior.

Why? Because of a passive husband who refused to lead and two disrespectful wives who didn't know the meaning of submission.

THE CLARKE MARRIAGE: ONE WIMP AND ONE WITCH

My name is Dave Clarke, and I was a wimp during the early years of my marriage. I'm man enough to admit it. I can relate to Jacob, except for having two wives with maidservants. I can barely handle one wife! But as a husband, I have been where Jacob was in terms of wimpiness.

Looking back, I'd say I was a passive wimp for the first six years of my marriage. With Sandy's urging, I did step up, early on, and do a decent number of chores. But I was way too focused on my education and career. I allowed (*forced* is more like it) Sandy to lead our home. She made all the decisions about money, the kids, and the home.

My primary goal was to get my doctorate in clinical psychology and build my career. I wasn't home much, and when I was, I was in my own little world. I avoided conflict with Sandy by giving in to whatever she wanted to do. My main contribution was playing with the kids.

Sandy lost more and more respect for me. She became colder and more critical. She nagged me to be home more, to take a more active role in the finances and in raising the kids, and to join her in making decisions. I didn't like her edgy, demeaning attitude and felt less of a man.

We were not as close as we'd been early in our marriage. We were pulling away from each other. Divorce was never in view, but we were definitely not on the right track.

We noticed that our relationship was suffering, and we

decided to do something about it. We began the process of change by doing two things. I have recommended these two things to hundreds of couples, and I am now recommending them to you and your spouse. First, have the guts to admit that your marriage has the pattern of a passive husband who won't lead and a disrespectful wife who won't submit. Or call it the Wimp and the Witch. You can fix it if you will admit to it.

Second, have a series of conversations about the sources of the Wimp and the Witch marital pattern. To kill a pattern, you have to understand what causes it.

THE WIMP SOURCES

Husband, if your dad was a wimp in his marriage, chances are very good that you're a wimp in your marriage. The modeling of a dad is extremely powerful in the life of a son. When you see your dad act like a wimp a million times with your mom, you are taught exactly how to carry out that role in your marriage.

If you were a momma's boy, you will likely choose a wife who will play that strong female role in your marriage. If your mother was the leader in your home, if she was in charge and called most of the shots, you're used to letting a woman control you. Join the club. Jacob was a momma's boy. Rebekah completely controlled Jacob, and he followed her leadership rather than the leadership of his father.

In America and most countries of the world, there is tremendous cultural pressure on men to be successful in the workplace. Career achievement is far and away the number one requirement of being a "real man." Being a workaholic is hardly considered shameful. It's expected. But, if you focus too much on your job, you automatically abdicate your leadership role in the home. You don't have the time or the energy left over from work to be the leader. And, if *you* don't lead, guess who will?

If you're a normal man, you have a natural tendency to avoid conflict with your wife. You hate fighting with her and do everything possible to avoid it. This usually means giving in and letting her have her way. Jacob gave in to his wives to avoid conflict and keep the peace. It didn't work, did it? It never does. Giving in to your wife strengthens her role as a leader, creates disrespect for you, and causes more conflict.

The Witch Sources

Wife, watching your dad play a passive wimp as you grew up had a major impact on you. You will probably look for a husband who is also passive. Or, maybe your dad was the opposite of passive. He was controlling, angry, and acted like a tyrant. His autocratic style wounded you, so you found an easygoing, much more passive man to marry.

If your mom was the leader in your home, you learned that role very well. You watched her make the key decisions for the family. You watched her nag your dad. You watched her show disrespect for him. You learned your lessons well and will mimic your strong mother's behavior as a wife. I know you won't want to hear this, but chances are very good that you are very much like your mother.

You really don't want to be the leader in your marriage. And yet, due to your husband's passivity and how you were raised, by default you have become the leader. Now you've been the leader for a while and you're used to the role. It's familiar. It's what you do every day. It has become a part of your identity. Even though you desire for your husband to lead, it's going to be hard to give up your authority and control.

Your lack of respect for your husband causes you to nag him and criticize him. You are trying to motivate him to change and to step up as the man in your home, but your negative approach actually drives him further away. Instead of motivating him, you make it less likely that he'll lead. Unwittingly, your poor attitude is feeding his passivity.

The Pattern Must Die

If you have the Wimp and the Witch pattern in your marriage, you must get rid of it. It is killing your intimacy. Admit that you have it and have several discussions about the sources of the Wimp and Witch roles. These steps will expose and weaken the pattern.

In the next chapters, I will teach you the leadership and submission skills necessary to eliminate this destructive pattern and replace it with security, respect, and closeness.

Outrageous Interaction

1. Discuss the Wimp and the Witch sources, and be honest about which ones apply to you.
2. If you have a version of the Wimp and the Witch pattern, admit it and agree to work together to kill it.

6
A Crash Course in Leadership

You cannot do what you have not been taught. Just ask Jacob. His father, Isaac, was a pathetically passive husband and parent. Isaac was a lightweight who allowed Jacob's mother, Rebekah, to call all the shots in their home. As a result, Rebekah had zero respect for Isaac and controlled him. Not a pretty picture.

Jacob learned in his home that the husband is a passive pipsqueak and the wife is a disrespectful controller. It was Isaac's job to teach Jacob how to be a leader in the home, but he obviously didn't get the job done. In fact, Isaac taught Jacob that the woman is the leader.

Is it any wonder that Jacob's marriages to Leah and Rachel turned out to be very similar to his mom and dad's marriage? Jacob had no clue how to lead a woman. He allowed Leah and Rachel to lead, while he played the role his dad taught him: the passive, controlled husband.

Maybe you weren't taught how to lead. Not having this skill has caused a lot of pain and unhappiness in your marriage. It's time for that to change.

Husband, I'm going to teach you the fundamentals of leadership. Your job as the leader is to meet your wife's needs, create and maintain regular Couple Talk Times, and *always* include her in decisions.

ASSUME NOTHING

If no obvious problems or disturbances are interrupting his comfortable lifestyle, a husband often will assume that his wife is happy and satisfied. He thinks to himself, *Hey, if she's cooking meals, doing the chores, taking care of the kids, and having sex with me, things must be okay.*

Husbands, in their selfish way, will make the following assumption: *If I'm happy, she's happy.* But it ain't necessarily so.

The light may begin to dawn if a man's wife holds a gun to his head and says, "It's all over, slimeball. I'm taking you out." At this point, the husband will realize that a problem exists. *Oh, I think she's a little unhappy with our relationship.*

Husband, do not assume your wife is happy and feeling loved. She could be dying inside. The fact that she continues to do the chores, cook, and have sex does not mean you are meeting her needs.

The typical husband truly believes he knows what his wife's needs are, and he's confident he's doing a terrific job meeting them. He's shocked to find out in my therapy office that he has no clue what her needs are and that he's not even close to meeting them.

I say the same thing to every husband I see in therapy: "Your *wife* defines whether or not you are meeting her needs. Not you! If she says you're not meeting her needs, you're not meeting her needs. The only way to know her needs is to *ask her. . .frequently.*"

ASK HER WHAT HER NEEDS ARE

Stop assuming you know what your wife's needs are. Not asking is like throwing darts in a pitch-black room. You have no idea where the dartboard is. You must ask her often. This wonderful creature's needs are varied, and they do change. Because she is a woman, she has strong emotions that dictate her needs. Her moods can change and are unpredictable. These are all good reasons why you will *not* know your wife's needs without asking.

Ask her in the morning before you go your separate ways for the day, "What can I do today to meet your needs?" When you ask, have a writing pad or electronic device handy and record what she says. You use lists for your job, don't you?

If you choose not to write down her needs, you are certain to forget. Now she'll be upset because not only are you not meeting her needs, but you can't even remember what they are. You'll be upset because she's upset. You'll have to spend time in the evening listening to her vent, telling her you're sorry forty-five times, and trying to reassure her that you love her. Or you can *write down* her needs and spend a pleasant evening with a warm, loving woman whose important, God-given, deep, female needs have been met by her loving husband. It's your choice.

Ask her in the evening as soon as you see her, "Sweetie, I love you. What can I do for you tonight?" *Jot down* her needs, and spend the first part of the evening taking care of them. With any luck, one of her requests may be, "Make wild love to me after the kids are in bed." (If you're asking for and meeting her needs on a daily basis, this kind of request won't be out of the question.)

Ask her just before bed, "Honey, is there anything I can do for you tomorrow?" Jot down what she says. That's a nice way to end the day.

Husband, I know what you're thinking: *Are you serious, Clarke? No husband I know asks for his wife's needs three times a day and writes them down.* No, I'm not kidding. True, very few husbands do what I am suggesting. Those who don't are the ones with unhappy, resentful, and cold wives. Those who do are the ones with happy, satisfied, and warm wives. Those who do are following the example of Jesus: "The Son of Man did not come to be served, but to serve" (Matthew 20:28).

SINCE YOU ARE THE MAN, BE THE MAN
Husband, I'll get right to the point. It's your job to lead the way to better communication. In fact, it's your job to lead your wife in every area of your relationship. I'm not telling you that. God is.

> *Wives, be subject to your own husbands, as to the Lord. For the husband is the head of the wife, as Christ also is the head of the church, He Himself being the Savior of the body. But as the church is subject to Christ, so also the wives ought to be to their husbands in everything.*
> EPHESIANS 5:22–24

Pretty clear, isn't it? God didn't leave any loopholes when assigning leadership in marriage.

If the wife leads in communication, it will never be efficient and successful—and that's *not* because women are not efficient or successful. It's because God made men and women different. Female leadership, giving the marriage and home direction, is not God's design. Both spouses are to be involved in the communication process, but God declares that the husband is to lead the way.

Husband, your first duty as communication leader is to create regular times to talk and make sure you have topics to discuss. You are responsible to sit down with your wife and schedule at least four thirty-minute Couple Talk Times each week. You are responsible to go to her and say, "It's time for our talk, honey."

WHAT DO WE TALK ABOUT?

Husband, you're also in charge of what happens during your Couple Talk Times. I don't mean you will be doing all the talking. You and your wife will both talk, and you will both listen. But, *you* will guide the content and the flow of the talk times. In other words, as the CEO, you run the meeting and determine the agenda.

Here's your crash course in how to run a Couple Talk Time.

CREATE SOME AMBIANCE

Meet with your wife in an atmosphere that is warm, soft, and inviting. This is more important to her than it is to you. Make sure the conversation area is clear of empty cups, wrappers, and miscellaneous clutter. Have some low-key music playing in the background, such as one of her favorite worship or other Christian CDs. Get her a cup of coffee, a mug of tea, or a soft drink. One or two candles burning wouldn't be a bad idea. Offer to give her a neck, back, or foot massage as you sit down and begin the meeting.

A Brief Prayer

Take her hand, and say a short prayer. It could be something like this: "Dear Father, thank You for my wonderful wife. Thank You for this time we have together. Please be with us and help us open up and really connect in conversation." This will automatically deepen the mood and help you both prepare to communicate.

Read Your Couples' Devotional

An easy and effective way to kick off communication is to read a page from a couples' devotional book and answer the questions at the end of the page. When you're just starting your Couple Talk Times, coming up with conversational material can be difficult. Reading a devotional page is a great conversation starter. My two favorite devotionals for couples are *Night Light* by James and Shirley Dobson, and *Moments Together for Couples* by Dennis and Barbara Rainey.

Husband, prepare by reading the devotional page a day or two before the meeting. Being a man, you may need time to digest the information and process it. *Jot down* your comments and reactions. This way, you'll have some things to say, and your wife will be impressed that you spent time preparing to talk with her.

Discuss with your wife your reactions to the devotional page, and answer the questions at the end. The devotional may trigger a stimulating conversation. Something in the text or in a question may lead to a deeper talk. If you find an interesting topic like this and want to talk about it again, make a note of it. Think about it for a day or so, and jot down your impressions and ideas. Then, at your next Couple Talk Time, you can continue the talk on the topic by sharing your notes.

Your wife will love the fact that you did some work on the topic, and she will have no trouble jumping into the conversation.

Carryover Topics

Next, you can segue into revisiting subjects of interest you've discussed in previous talk times or in other conversations. This is the Carryover Principle: talking about the same topic two, three, or four times to achieve a deeper level of emotional intimacy.

Whether you bring up one of these carryover topics or your wife does, you can refer to your notes and say, "Yes, we talked about that on Monday and agreed to continue that talk today. I thought more about it, and I wrote down some things that occurred to me."

If you don't have notes, you'll sit there like the village idiot with absolutely nothing to say. "What? Are you sure we talked about that?" With notes, you'll sit there like a man who cares enough about his wife to remember topics of conversation and actually prepares to talk about them. You'll go from being a poor conversationalist to a caring conversationalist.

A poor conversationalist gets no respect, no intimacy; he gets disappointment, maybe even disgust, and mediocre sex (if your wife is even willing to have sex). The caring conversationalist gets warmth, love, intimacy, respect, and better and more frequent sex. So, who do you want to be?

If you and your wife decide to continue talking about a carryover topic, make a note of it.

CURRENT EVENTS

After getting a little deeper into one or two carryover topics, you can bring up new material: work, kids, home maintenance, social plans, friends and family, church, and events of interest that have occurred since your last Couple Talk Time.

If any of these prove stimulating and promise more intimacy, agree to carry them over to the next talk time. Jot down these topics for processing.

PRAYER TOGETHER

Make a list of prayer requests on a pad. You can call this your prayer pad. Divide the list and pray out loud, one at a time, for the items on the list. The wife prays for the two or three items she selects, and then the husband prays for his items. Husband, make sure you hold your wife's hand during this five-minute prayer time. If you're in crisis or have a pressing concern, you'll pray for more than five minutes. Remember to thank God for who He is, for His many blessings, and for His presence and help in your Couple Talk Time.

PRAYER TO CONVERSATION

When you finish praying, you will naturally talk about some of the issues you just lifted up to God. We tend to pray for the most urgent concerns of our hearts, and following up on these topics in conversation can lead to greater emotional intimacy.

One more time to make sure you get it: if you identify a carryover topic that comes up during your talk time, jot it down *immediately*.

This progression I've explained is not set in concrete. However, it has proven very helpful to many couples who are beginning the Couple Talk Time program. Most important, after it helps you *start* the process, it also provides structure, a nice flow, and multiple opportunities for deeper conversations. Try it, and see how it goes. Play with the order of steps and mix it up to find a sequence that works best for both of you. Every now and then, change the order to keep things fresh.

Conversational intimacy is unpredictable. So, in every talk time, the sequence of steps is subject to change. If you hit on a winning topic and are building an interesting conversation, go with it. Pursuing a potentially intimate conversation is more important than covering all the steps in the Couple Talk Time progression.

ALWAYS INCLUDE HER IN DECISIONS

Always, always, always ask your wife for input before making a significant decision. Consider your wife's viewpoint, her wisdom, her talents and abilities, and her intuition. She's your equal partner in the relationship, so treat her as an equal.

Besides, how can you expect her to support you in a decision that she had no part in making?

It's demeaning, insulting, and a failure in servant leadership to make decisions without consulting your wife.

Involve your wife in the family finances. She needs to know where every penny is. Make financial decisions together. Major purchases, the development of a budget, investments, and tithing all require her input. I know husbands who tell their wives nothing about the money. Why? Is it a secret? Are you in the CIA? Tell her! Keep her involved.

I know this is a lot of information to take in. Have a series of conversations, during your four thirty-minute Couple Talk Times each week, and discuss how you are doing as a leader. Ask your wife what one specific action you can take in the next two weeks to improve as you assess your leadership. In your Couple Talk Time, talk about your ongoing progress in this area. When you master that particular skill, add another, and work on that one for two weeks. Keep going until you have achieved success in all the areas covered in this chapter. With time, practice, and working together, I guarantee you will become outrageously good at the role of leader. God will be pleased that you are living out your biblical role of husband, and your marriage relationship will be greatly improved.

Outrageous Interaction

1. Specifically, what did your parents teach you about leadership? What kind of leader was your dad?
2. Husband, ask your wife to tell you the things you are doing well as a leader. Ask her what things you can improve in your role as leader.
3. Talk specifically about the three areas of leadership covered in this chapter. Honestly evaluate yourself in these areas. How do you think you're doing? How does your wife think you're doing?
4. Follow my recommendation to work on one leadership skill every two weeks, evaluating your progress in your Couple Talk Times.

7
A Crash Course in Submission

Wives, now it's your turn. Submission is every bit as important as leadership to the success of a marriage. Just as your husband wasn't taught to be a leader, you probably weren't taught to be submissive. You can join Leah and Rachel in the "we weren't taught submission" club. And it's a club with a lot of members.

Leah and Rachel came from a home where submission to the husband was nonexistent. Their father, Laban, was a conniving, manipulative, selfish user. He sounds a lot like Jacob, doesn't he? Laban was totally in control of his home. It seems likely that his wife was a compliant doormat. The Bible doesn't even mention her name.

Laban selfishly used both Leah and Rachel to get what he wanted from Jacob. He forced Leah to marry a man who didn't love her, and he forced Rachel to wait fourteen years before her marriage to Jacob was finalized (Genesis 29:15–30). His treatment of his precious daughters was shameful. It was also emotionally abusive and left them traumatized. And I think it made them determined never to allow a man to dominate and wound them again.

Leah and Rachel came into marriage without the slightest idea of how to submit to their husband. They'd been taught never to trust a man. They'd been taught never to respect a man. They'd been taught that manipulation was the only way to get their needs met. So, both Leah and Rachel didn't trust Jacob, didn't respect him, and manipulated him to get what they wanted.

I'm here to teach you the fundamentals of submission, because you cannot do what you have not been taught to do.

Here's what submission is *not*: Wives, your job as a submissive wife is to give your husband sex on demand, wait on him hand and foot, and immediately obey his every instruction. This kind of submission, which is taught in many churches, isn't even close to a biblical definition.

A truly submissive wife does three things: she meets her husband's needs, uses one-way communication (which I will discuss later in this chapter), and allows her husband to be the leader in the marriage relationship.

GIVE HIM RESPECT

Every husband has a deep need for his wife's respect. Scripture is clear about respecting your man (Ephesians 5:33; 1 Peter 3:1–2, 6). You can meet this need in two primary ways.

First, do not criticize, belittle, or nag him. These verbal slaps are not merely ineffective motivators, they are damaging, disrespectful barbs that strike at the heart of his manhood. When you cut him verbally or remind him over and over to do something, you are acting like the "contentious woman" Solomon talks about in Proverbs:

> It is better to live in a corner of a roof than in a house shared with a contentious woman.
>
> PROVERBS 21:9

That's exactly where your smart, feisty mouth will drive him: to the corner of the roof.

Submission does *not* mean that you do not express your feelings to your husband. But when you have something to say to him, say it in the right way, in private, adult to adult, firmly and honestly, without sarcasm or attacking him as a person. If you're angry, express that anger clearly and concisely without being mean. If you are hurt, express clearly your *hurt*; *don't* express it in the form of anger. As Scripture teaches, speak the truth in love (Ephesians 4:15).

Second, praise your man often. To get a good picture of how to praise him and how often, read the Old Testament book of Song of Solomon. Shulamith showed her deep respect for Solomon by praising him frequently. When I say frequently, I mean frequently. Be like Shulamith, and your husband will feel respected. And he'll be motivated to love you in the ways you want to be loved.

Praise him for who he is, for his character, for working at his job, for jobs he does around the home, for spending time with the children, for his physical attractiveness (see Shulamith's use of "young stag" in Song of Solomon 2:9, 17 and 8:14), and for his efforts to lead you and the family spiritually. At a bare minimum, try hard to praise him for a specific quality or behavior every day. Two or three compliments per day would be even better.

GIVE HIM FOOD

Your husband loves food. It's not just a physical need either. When you feed him well, he feels loved by you. He will be drawn to you emotionally as the one who feeds him. His stomach and his heart are connected. I know this sounds crude and simplistic, but we are talking about a man. Keep your cupboards stocked with his favorite snacks. Be willing to go to his kind of restaurant at least on every other date. Make as many home-cooked meals as your schedule will allow. Ask him what he'd like for these meals.

GIVE HIM TOUCH

Just about every husband I've ever talked to wants and needs more physical affection from his wife. More sex too, but I'll save that topic for another chapter. Your husband needs you to touch him on a daily basis. I'm talking about significant nonsexual touching: kissing, hugging, neck and foot and back massages, running your fingers through his hair, scalp massages, and making out on the couch or in the bedroom.

Touch communicates love to him and builds up his masculine self-esteem. Touching him can also lower his walls and help him open up in your Couple Talk Times. When Sandy gives me a five-minute foot massage at the beginning of a talk time, I'm putty in her hands. I feel her love, I feel relaxed and confident, and I feel like listening better and talking more. I also feel like having sex, but I control myself, because we need to have a talk time first!

I've seen wives who give more affection and better hugs and kisses to their pets than to their husbands. You might say you're just not an affectionate person. I say, fine. Get over it. Work hard at being affectionate with your husband at least once a day. It's not optional. He needs your physical touch.

ONE-WAY COMMUNICATION

In one-way communication, you *briefly* tell your husband your views, your thoughts, and your emotions about a topic, and *do not expect an immediate reply*. I call it one-way, because you do all the talking.

Tell him that he doesn't have to respond. Ask him to listen and concentrate in order to understand, to take time to process what you've said, and then, when he's ready, to share his reaction. When you're done talking, you either walk away or simply go silent. If you're with him at home in a Couple Talk Time, in the car, in a restaurant, or out somewhere else, just be quiet for at least five minutes. You can continue in silence or bring up another topic of conversation.

In other words, speak your piece, and then move on. Unlike what you may have done in the past, do not press him for an immediate reaction. Why not? Two reasons. First, most men cannot respond right away. They need time to process and figure out their feelings and thoughts on an issue. Personal issues require even more time. Second, men will always clam up when they feel pressured by women. They feel controlled, and they demonstrate with their silence that no one can make them talk.

If you express yourself in *five minutes or less* and allow him time to process his response, you will increase the likelihood that your man will consider what you say and get back to you to continue the conversation. If you nag him, or even if you ask him sweetly for a quick response, he will most likely freeze up and may never respond on that topic. Never.

The way I'm suggesting, using the one-way communication strategy, will get you a *maybe*. Your way, the natural female way of pushing him to say something back right away, will get you a *never*. Try it my way.

One-way communication comes in different shapes and sizes. Let's look at several.

THE FIVE-MINUTE BURST DURING COUPLE TALK TIMES

For regular, no-conflict Couple Talk Times, try the five-minute, one-way burst. As you begin speaking, ask your husband right up front to listen and to reflect back to you what he hears. As you talk, check in with him periodically to make sure he's engaged with you: "Are you with me, honey?" "Do you understand what I'm saying?" "What emotion do you think I'm feeling right now?" You're not asking for his response to what you're saying. You're seeing if he understands the basic content and your emotions about what you are saying.

Talk for five minutes and then stop. Give him a chance to think, to digest what you've said, and to prepare some kind of response. He might say something back, or he might not. At least by pausing, you're giving him an opportunity to connect with you.

If he says nothing during your pause, let five minutes go by. Don't jump right back in with more comments on the same topic. Talk about another topic for five minutes, and pause again. If he doesn't respond, let ten minutes go by. By being silent more often, you might motivate him to initiate more conversations. He'll notice your silence and may talk more to draw you closer to him.

At the end of your thirty-minute talk time, tell him the one or two topics you'd like him to process and get back to you about. This is the best way to remind him that you want to hear what he has to say on these topics.

THE FIVE-MINUTE BURST AT OTHER TIMES

Obviously, you and your husband will talk outside of the four Couple Talk Times each week. In these times, make sure you have his full attention. Then talk for five minutes or less about your desired topic. Tell him you'd like him to think about what you've said and get back to you with his response when he's ready. Tell him he can respond before your next scheduled Couple Talk Time (you should be so lucky), or he can wait until the talk time.

THE THIRTY-SECOND BURST WHEN HE FAILS TO RESPOND

What if you use one-way communication and he still doesn't come back to you with a response? Well, he is a man, and that's certainly going to happen a lot. When you've waited a day or two and he clearly has no intention of giving you a response, try a two-step follow-up.

First, give him a low-key, no-emotion reminder. You only get one. If you remind him twice, you're a nagging witch. In thirty seconds or less, say something like this: "Remember that issue we discussed? When you're ready, I'd like you to find me and give me your reaction to what I said." After this statement, say nothing else about it. Move on.

If he still won't talk about it, go to Step Two—a one-way communication that expresses your feelings about his decision to ignore you and refuse to respond to the topic. Say something like this: "I'm angry and disappointed that you've chosen not to come back to me about (whatever issue you brought up). That makes me feel unloved and unimportant. I wanted you to know." Then drop it and walk away. Don't bring it up again.

This second step is designed to cleanse your system of anger and resentment; it allows you to forgive him and gives you closure on the issue. And maybe he will feel bad and come back to you with a response to the issue.

THE THIRTY-SECOND BURST WHEN HE DOESN'T WANT TO TALK

He's obviously upset about something. You ask him a reasonable question: "What's wrong?" He replies, "Nothing." Instead of yelling "Liar!" give him a thirty-second burst of one-way communication, gently and lovingly expressed, with words like these: "Look, I know something's wrong. I know it's hard for you to talk about it, so I won't try to pry it out of you. I want to comfort and support you, but I can't if you don't tell me what's bothering you. When you want to share what it is, come to me. You can share it a little at a time over several days, and I'll just listen and reflect back to you what I'm hearing."

ALLOW YOUR HUSBAND TO BE THE LEADER

Submission means allowing your husband to be the leader in your relationship and yielding to his authority. Not because he is superior. Not because he is more intelligent. Not because he has more ability. But because this is the role that God commands him to fulfill. Here's how to empower, encourage, and help your husband take on his role as leader.

WALK CLOSE TO GOD

It is only with God's power, through the Holy Spirit (who lives in you and wants to control you and empower you to live the Christian life), that you can truly submit. If it's just you in your own power trying to submit, you'll never be able to do it. It's humanly impossible. Just like a husband loving his wife as Christ loves the church, wifely submission is a God thing. You submit with God's help, or you don't submit at all. You don't submit for your husband. You submit for God.

> *Wives, be subject to your own husbands, as to the Lord.*
> EPHESIANS 5:22

> *Wives, be subject to your husbands, as is fitting in the Lord.*
> COLOSSIANS 3:18

Don't focus on your husband as you submit. Keep your eyes on the Lord. You're doing it for Him. And He will bless you for your act of obedience and love (John 14:15).

As an Equal Partner, Speak Your Mind Freely

Openly sharing your feelings and opinions on significant decisions and issues is a crucial part of your role as a submissive wife. Always. God wants you to offer your husband guidance and feedback: "Then the LORD God said, 'It is not good for the man to be alone; I will make him a helper suitable for him'" (Genesis 2:18). As a helper to your husband, you are to tell him in a loving and honest and firm way what you think is best in every important situation. That's being helpful. That's what a helper does.

Be like the Proverbs 31 wife: "She opens her mouth in wisdom, and the teaching of kindness is on her tongue" (Proverbs 31:26). You have wisdom that no one else has—about your husband, your children, and your home. You need to share that wisdom. Your husband may not always want to hear what you have to say. That's too bad. He should. Lay it on him anyway. That's your job. That's obeying the Lord and following His plan.

Follow the Leader

Allow your husband to make decisions in the key areas of life, and follow them unless they clearly violate God's revealed will through His written word, the Bible. If you are making a major decision, talk about it a number of times over several days (or several weeks), fully sharing your views about the situation. Pray together about the decision. And then allow your husband to decide what to do. Support him and the approach he wants to take—whether you agree or not.

Husband, the only time your decision should run counter to your wife's opinion and feelings is when you can honestly say something like this: "Honey, I have thought long and hard about this. I have prayed continually for God's guidance. I've read whatever I can that the Bible says about this. I've listened thoroughly to you and your expression of your feelings and ideas. I've asked a couple of good and godly men about their experience and for their opinions. As far as I can discern, I believe this is what we should do."

Wife, if your husband is sinning, do *not* submit. Confront his sin and take action against it. If he asks you to do something that would go against biblical principles, do not submit. Refuse to sin for him.

I know this is just as much information for you to take in as the leadership chapter was for your husband. It will take time to learn these skills. Have a series of conversations—during your four thirty-minute Couple Talk Times each week—and discuss how you are doing in your role of submission. Ask your husband what one specific action you can take in the next two weeks to improve as a submissive wife. In your Couple Talk Times, talk about your ongoing progress in this area or the others I've mentioned. When you master one particular skill, add another and work on that one for two weeks. Keep going until you have achieved success in all the areas covered in this chapter.

With time and practice and working together, I firmly believe you can become an outrageously good, submissive wife. It's what God wants. It's what your husband wants. It's an essential ingredient in an outrageously great marriage.

Outrageous Interaction

1. Specifically, what did your parents teach you or model for you about submission? What kind of submissive wife was your mom?
2. Ask your husband to tell you the things you are doing well as a submissive wife. Ask him what things you can improve as a submissive wife.
3. Talk specifically about the three areas of submission I cover in this chapter. Honestly evaluate yourself in these areas. How do you think you're doing? How does your husband think you're doing?
4. Follow my recommendation to work on one submission skill every two weeks, evaluating your progress in your Couple Talk Times.

8
Don't Get a Divorce Unless You Have a Very Good Reason

*"Do you take _____ to be your lawfully wedded wife,
to live together in holy matrimony? Do you promise
to love, comfort, honor, and keep her for better or
worse, for richer or poorer, in sickness and in health,
and forsaking all others, be faithful only to her, so
long as you both shall live?"*
"I do."
*"Do you take _____ to be your lawfully wedded hus-
band, to live together in holy matrimony? Do you
promise to love, comfort, honor, and keep him for
better or worse, for richer or poorer, in sickness
and in health, and forsaking all others, be faithful
only to him, so long as you both shall live?"*
"I do."

These are serious words of a sacred covenant. God created the institution of marriage (Genesis 2:20–25). The union of husband and wife is the very picture of the relationship between Jesus Christ and the church (Ephesians 5:22–33). Jesus plainly stated that marriage is designed by God to be a permanent, lifelong relationship (Matthew 19:1–12; Mark 10:1–12). If you're wondering how God feels about divorce, read Malachi 2:16: "'I hate divorce,' says the LORD, the God of Israel."

SO LONG AS YOU BOTH SHALL LIVE?
Wedding vows used to mean something—*everything*. In today's world, they mean less and less. As revealed in survey after survey, the divorce rate in the United States stands at 50 percent. That's 50 percent of all married couples.

Tragically, it includes those who have a personal relationship with Jesus Christ as well as those who do not. Having a relationship with Jesus doesn't seem to make a difference in terms of staying married. It should, of course. But it doesn't. At least, it doesn't for many Christians who get divorced.

Why do some spouses, both Christians and non-Christians, choose to end their marriages? Some have sound, biblical reasons for divorce, but the vast majority are acting selfishly and are deceiving themselves into thinking they have a good reason to kill their marriage. As a Christian psychologist who specializes in marital therapy and who presents marriage seminars across the United States, I've had a front-row seat for twenty-five years, watching spouses explain why they want to get a divorce.

I think I've heard every possible lame excuse for ending a marriage. Early in my career, I would listen quietly to these excuses and try to gently talk the excuse giver out of divorce. That didn't work very well. So, for the past twenty years, I have assertively refuted every poor excuse for ending a marriage that I've heard. This tough, in-your-face approach honors the sacredness of marriage, supports the spouse who doesn't want to divorce, and changes the minds of some spouses who want out.

Here are the top outrageous marriage-killing excuses I've heard and my typical responses.

Speaking Truth to Powerful Stupidity
Stupid Excuse: I don't love you anymore.

Dave: Wow! Poof! Your love just disappeared one day? It's gone because you stopped feeding/caring for it, nurturing it over time. Your spouse contributed to this tragedy, but so did you. Tell me what you did in your marriage to kill your love for your spouse.

Stupid Excuse: We've grown apart.

Dave: That happens to all couples. Join the club. Jobs, male-female differences, annoying habits, stress, and kids can cause a couple to grow apart. So? You can choose to grow back together and keep growing together.

Stupid Excuse: I never loved you.

Dave: Baloney! You loved your spouse. That's why you got married. You didn't have an arranged marriage, did you? You are attempting to rewrite history to justify divorce. Even if you're telling the truth, don't you think God can change your heart and give you back your love for your spouse?

Stupid Excuse: I felt pressured to marry you.

Dave: It was awful, wasn't it? Being tied up, drugged, and dragged to the altar must have been traumatic. Show me the wedding picture of you with the shotgun to your head. Give me a break. You got married because you were in love and you wanted to get married. Is it pressure now—again—that makes you want a divorce? If you choose divorce, you are going to feel some real pressure—from God, in whose presence you swore never to forsake your spouse.

Stupid Excuse: We've become diffcrent persons.

Dave: Really? When exactly did it dawn on you that you married a person of the *opposite* sex, someone very *different* from you? Boy, that must have been a shock! Of course you're different! Incredibly different! That's true for every couple! Not only are you different, but it will be normal for you both to change as the years go by. What you have to learn is how to adjust to your differences and make them work for you.

Stupid Excuse: People can't change.

Dave: You're talking to a clinical psychologist, so you might want to come up with a better excuse. I'm in the business of change. With God's power and the hard work of individuals, I see men and women change significantly all the time. And, *with God, nothing is impossible* (Matthew 19:26; Luke 1:37).

Stupid Excuse: I feel trapped.

Dave: What? Has your spouse chained you to a chair in your home? An unhappy marriage can produce this feeling, but it can be fixed.

Stupid Excuse: I need space.

Dave: You already have plenty of space—between your ears. You want more? If you wanted space, why didn't you stay single? Go ahead and say what you really mean: "I want to do sinful behaviors that I can't do while I'm married." At least that would be honest.

Stupid Excuse: I need to find myself.

Dave: Let me see if I can help you. You're married. You have kids, and you have responsibilities. That's you. If you leave your marriage based on this ridiculous excuse, you'll find yourself in sin and misery. God wants you to work on your individual issues and save your marriage.

Stupid Excuse: It's not you; it's me.

Dave: Now, that makes sense. It *is* you. You're a mess, and you're not thinking clearly or rationally. Let's work on what's wrong with you before you ruin your whole life and severely damage those who love and need you.

Stupid Excuse: I'm just not good for you.

Dave: Right now, that's true. You are wounding your spouse with your selfish behavior. You're also not good for yourself; without realizing it, you are doing horrible damage to yourself.

Stupid Excuse: You're not stimulating intellectually.

Dave: Please! What are you, some kind of genius? I doubt you can find anyone of the opposite sex who can be on your superior level of intelligence. Please show me the Nobel Prizes you've won. For such a brilliant person, you're acting like a moron.

Stupid Excuse: I've grown beyond you.

Dave: No, I don't think so. You're acting like a spoiled, immature, and irresponsible adolescent. I know quite a few teenagers who act more mature than you do.

Stupid Excuse: I'm having a midlife crisis.

Dave: Well then, I guess you can't help it! Your midlife crisis is your free ticket to all these sinful, destructive actions. However, if you choose, you can work through your personal issues without damaging your spouse and ruining your marriage and your life. If you think you're in a crisis now, just wait until after you divorce your spouse. God's going to give you a whopper of a crisis to bring you back to your senses and back to Him (Hebrews 12:5–7).

Stupid Excuse: I love you like a brother (or sister).

Dave: That's just insulting. And not even true. A sibling loves more deeply than you do now and would never treat someone the way you are treating the person to whom you pledged a lifetime of love. You can get your passion back if you lean on God and do the hard work I ask you to do.

Stupid Excuse: I love you as the parent of our children.

Dave: No, you don't. That sounds nice, but it's a lie. You don't love your spouse at all. And you don't love your kids either. If you truly loved your children, you'd work on your marriage and not give them a legacy of loss, hurt, confusion, and abandonment.

Stupid Excuse: I love you, but I'm not *in* love with you.

Dave: But you are in love with yourself, what you want, what will please you, aren't you? Every couple loses that *in love* feeling. With the right steps and relying on God's power and the strength He gives, you will get it back again.

Stupid Excuse: I don't love you the way a spouse should love you.

Dave: Yeah, you've got that right. God wants your next statement to be: "And I'm going to do whatever it takes to love you the way I should love you." Will you obey God and do your best to build a real love for your spouse?

Stupid Excuse: God wants me to be happy.

Dave: No, He doesn't. Show me where in the Bible it says that God wants you to be happy. As a matter of information, the Bible states that there is pleasure in sin; but the sad truth is that it passes away quickly and is always temporary (Hebrews 11:25). According to the Bible, God is not interested in your happiness. He is interested in your holiness (1 Thessalonians 4:3; Hebrews 12:14). What He wants is for you to obey Him and work on your marriage. He promises that will bring you *joy*, which is a lot better than happiness (John 15:10–11). Ironically, if you get a divorce for unbiblical reasons, you will be the opposite of happy. No one breaks God's laws and gets away with it.

Stupid Excuse: It's better for the kids, because our bad marriage is hurting them.

Dave: A bad marriage is better than no marriage at all and—in most cases—better than the loss of an involved dad or mom. Kids of all ages are deeply, *permanently* wounded by divorce. I don't recommend you stay in a bad marriage. I recommend—for the sake of the children especially—that you work on your marriage and improve it. This shows— *proves*—immense love for your children and would truly be what is better for them.

Stupid Excuse: I don't feel anything for my spouse. I'm numb.

Dave: Don't panic. Numb happens. Dumb happens too. You're dumb if you divorce for this excuse. Decide to hang in there and work on your relationship. Your feelings will come back better and deeper than ever.

Stupid Excuse: For years I've tolerated a lack of love and my needs not being met. Now I'm exhausted and beyond frustration, and I'm done.

Dave: It's your fault for stuffing your feelings all those years and not expressing those feelings about how unhappy you were. Now that you finally have your spouse's attention and real change can happen, you're walking out? Give yourself and your spouse a chance, and let's see what happens.

Stupid Excuse: I've fallen in love with someone else. This person is my soul mate.

Dave: Try "sin mate." You are committing adultery, and God will never bless this sinful, disgusting relationship. If you turn from it, God will forgive you and help you develop a genuine love with your spouse.

All these stupid excuses are culturally acceptable ways of saying, "I'm a selfish pig, and I want a divorce so I can do what I want to do." Of course, it doesn't sound good to say that, so these "I want a divorce" spouses use excuses that make them feel better about themselves.

All these excuses are pathetic, distorted attempts to rationalize a sinful choice. When I tell people what I think of these excuses, they don't like me very much. In addition to exposing and mocking their flimsy lies, I add, "That's not a biblical reason for divorce. And if it's not biblical, it's not good enough."

I guess it's pretty obvious that if you see me in therapy, you'd better have a very good reason for getting a divorce.

THERE ARE GOOD REASONS FOR GETTING A DIVORCE

In my opinion, there are two biblical reasons for divorce: *adultery* (Matthew 5:32; 19:9) and *physical desertion* (1 Corinthians 7:15).

Let me be unambiguous. I have never recommended divorce, and I never will, even when there is a biblical reason to end the marriage. With the right action steps and God's help, any marriage can be saved and made into a great relationship. Divorce is none of my business. God must make that decision evident to you.

What do you do if your spouse is involved in serious sin and refuses to stop that sin? Your spouse is physically and/or sexually abusing you. Emotionally abusing you with vicious, hurtful words. Your spouse is a sex addict, an alcoholic, or drug addict. A gambler. Your spouse refuses to provide financial support. Your spouse refuses to do anything to improve the marriage.

I recommend to the other spouse a strong, tough-love approach, based on Matthew 18:15–17. (In this chapter, and in chapters 17 and 18, I will refer often to these verses.) This passage teaches three stages of confrontation followed by separation due to the failure of the sinning party to acknowledge his or her sin. If your sinning spouse still remains in sin, then I urge you to seek God's direction as to whether the marriage ought to be ended. God will show you what to do. (In chapters 17 and 18, I describe in detail what you need to do if your spouse is in serious sin.)

Bottom line: God expects you to do your best to stay married and to work on your marriage. No matter how bad your marriage is now, it can become a God-centered, wonderfully fulfilling, intimate relationship. Do not quit unless you have a biblical reason to quit and have done all you can to save and rebuild your marriage.

JACOB, LEAH, AND RACHEL NEVER QUIT

You have already read chapter 5, so you know that Jacob's marriages to Leah and Rachel were not shining examples of marital bliss. Far from it. Those two marriages were lousy. Wait. *Lousy* is not a strong enough word. *Awful* is a better, more descriptive word. Awful. Awful. Awful.

Jacob did not love Leah. He did nothing to try to create love for her. He never loved her, not even a little. Leah lived in a constant state of rejection. All her attempts to make Jacob love her failed. All she had was her children. I'd call that an awful marriage. Are you a wife whose husband doesn't love you? Or a husband whose wife doesn't love you?

Leah and Rachel engaged in a vicious, no-holds-barred baby-making competition. They both were controlling, manipulating schemers who would do anything to achieve their goals. Jacob, who was passive, weak, and preoccupied with nonpriorities, allowed these two drama queens to dominate him, even agreeing to have sex with their maidservants. This may have been culturally acceptable, but it was morally abhorrent and a disaster for the marriages.

These two marriages were filled with all kinds of nasty conflicts. Turmoil and misery reigned. There was no trust. No respect. No peace. No intimacy. Jacob, Leah, and Rachel starred in the world's first soap opera. But for them it wasn't acting. These were real people in two really bad marriages.

Despite being so miserable, Jacob and Leah and Rachel did not quit. They hung in there and stayed married. Back in that day, the husband was the only spouse with the authority to end a marriage. Despite not loving Leah, Jacob stayed married to her. Despite Rachel's not returning his love, Jacob stayed married to her. Despite all their manipulating and deceiving and controlling behavior, Jacob stayed married to both his wives.

Every couple needs this kind of *outrageous perseverance*, because marriage is hard. There will be times when both you and your spouse will feel utterly frustrated, hurt, and hopeless. You will want to walk away from your marriage. Don't do it. Dig down deep and find the outrageous perseverance that Jacob, Leah, and Rachel demonstrated. God expects you to persevere, and He will honor you for doing so.

Do Not Quit. Instead, Work on Your Marriage

As important as perseverance is to a marriage, don't just persevere in yours. Staying married but being miserable isn't what God desires for you. God wants your marriage to be great, no matter how bad it might be now. God is not glorified by a long-term, lousy marriage. God is glorified when two spouses don't quit and work very hard to build a new, intimate marriage.

Keep in mind that you have so many more resources to

build your marriage than Jacob, Leah, and Rachel had. If you have a personal relationship with God, then the Holy Spirit of God, God Himself, dwells in you (1 Corinthians 6:19), and His enabling power awaits your asking. If you attend a church (and I hope you do), you have a loving pastor and a built-in group of supporters. You can read terrific books on marriage (like this one, if I do say so myself). You have access to Christian counselors who are trained to help you heal from past mistakes and learn how to be intimate with your spouse.

If your marriage is in trouble, it's very important that you begin taking action to address the problems—right now. If you don't, your problems will get worse and worse and worse. Eventually, one of you will "hit the wall" and want out of the marriage. Don't delay taking action.

Specifically, I have four steps I want you to follow. It's ideal and best if you and your spouse take these steps together. If your spouse refuses to work on the marriage with you, go ahead and follow these steps on your own. Before each step, ask your spouse to do it with you. If he or she refuses, do the step yourself. Your actions may motivate your spouse to join you in the process. Even if your spouse never chooses to join you, you will know that you did everything possible to save your marriage.

STEP ONE: READ THIS BOOK

I know you're already reading this book. So you're already ahead of the game. I believe the accounts of these ten biblical couples teach the relationship skills you need to build a good marriage. Read each chapter with your spouse, talk about what you're reading, answer the end-of-chapter questions together, and apply the principles.

Although all these biblical couples supply valuable marital tools, you will relate to some couples more than others. Zero in on those examples and spend more time working on the principles they teach.

Step Two: Turn to God, and Lean on Him

I don't know how to state this truth gently and subtly, so I'm just going to lay it on you. Humanly speaking, marriage is impossible. I'm not kidding. Men and women are too incredibly different to understand each other; to communicate, recognize, understand, and meet real needs; and to experience a truly deep love. For years, Sandy and I tried in our own power to build a great marriage, and we failed. When we asked God for help and relied on Him, our marriage reached the level of closeness and passion we'd always wanted.

To get God's help, you need to *have a personal relationship with Him, through Jesus Christ*. In chapter 2, I explained how to do this. If you don't have this personal relationship, and you're ready to begin one now, reread the "You Both Must Be Christians" section in chapter 2, and pray the simple prayer.

Being in marital crisis is a good time to reach out to God and start a relationship with Him. The very second you and God are connected, He will begin providing you with the power and ability to make your marriage work.

I strongly recommend that you *regularly attend a local church*. The church is God's chosen vehicle to change the world. The local church can also play a huge role in changing your personal life and your marriage. A local church can stimulate your spiritual growth and vitality. It's where you can find a small group, Sunday school class, or marriage ministry. Right now, you need a spiritual and relationship "hospital" where you can be helped to grow closer to God and to your spouse.

This is also a very good time to *start praying together as a couple*. Praying together regularly will bring you closer spiritually and emotionally. It will connect you as a couple to God and allow you to use His power to work on your marital problems. Reread the "How to Pray" section in chapter 2 for specific guidelines on praying as a couple.

STEP THREE: REACH OUT FOR HUMAN HELP

Set up a meeting with the pastor of the church you attend. Sit down with him, and tell him about your marital struggles. A pastor can provide unique encouragement, spiritual motivation, and prayer support. Even one meeting can be a powerful boost to your hope for building a new marriage. The pastor may not continue to counsel you personally, but he'll be on the team. He'll pray for you, check in on you, and be able to refer you to a mentor couple and a Christian counselor (see below).

With your pastor's help, try to find a *mentor couple*. A mentor couple is a married couple who are followers of Jesus Christ; have a solid, Christian, healthy, and intimate marriage; and are willing to come alongside you and your spouse to help you toward a better marriage. This couple will meet with you regularly to teach marital skills, provide spiritual and emotional support, hold you accountable as you work to improve, and pray with you. They will also be available by phone in times of crisis.

This mentor couple may be your pastor and his wife (if they have time with their other, primary duties) or another couple in the church. If you can't find a mentor couple, find a married follower of Jesus of your same sex to be your confidant(e) and accountability partner. Choose a friend, not a family member.

Finally, and very importantly, find *an experienced Christian therapist* for couple counseling. Ask your pastor for a name or call Focus on the Family (1-800-A-FAMILY) and get a list of Christian therapists in your area. As helpful as your pastor and mentor couple can be, you may need a specialist to guide you through the healing and recovery process.

STEP FOUR: DO YOUR BEST

Do your very best to save and rebuild your marriage. Because marriage is a sacred relationship, this is what God wants you to do. Act as if you are trying to save your own life from a serious, even deadly disease. Even if your spouse refuses to change,

God will honor and bless you for doing your best on your own to build a new marriage.

Outrageous Interaction

1. Talk about your wedding day and the vows (the solemn promises) you made to each other. Who was in the audience listening to your vows? What was the most precious thing to you about that day? Will you recommit yourself to keep the vows you made for a lifetime?

2. If you have been divorced, talk to your spouse about that marriage or those marriages, your mistakes, your ex-spouse's mistakes, what you've learned from the experience, how the marriage ended, any regrets you carry, and any leftover pain you feel.

3. If you ended a marriage for unbiblical reasons, tell your spouse what happened. Confess your mistakes, and with your spouse pray and ask for God's forgiveness for disobeying Him.

4. If you are unhappy in your marriage, admit this to your spouse right now, and tell him or her why you are unhappy. Do this without any personal attacks. Agree that together you will follow my four steps to marital recovery. If your spouse refuses, go ahead and take the steps on your own.

Solomon and Shulamith

OUTRAGEOUS COMMUNICATION, REJECTION, AND PASSION

9
"Baby, Talk to Me"

When you walk down the aisle after being pronounced husband and wife, your passion is at 100 percent. You are madly in love. You have married the perfect person and the future is unbelievably bright, sunny, and wonderful. What could go wrong?

Actually, because you're married and living together 24-7, quite a bit can go wrong. Quite a bit *will* go wrong. And you won't have to wait long for it to happen. Within a matter of months, maybe even weeks, your passion starts taking hits.

You realize that your spouse has a number of incredibly annoying habits. Your passion goes down to 90 percent. You discover that your spouse has weaknesses and that those weaknesses cause your needs to go unmet. Your passion goes down to 80 percent. You find out that you and your spouse have tremendous differences in just about every area. Your passion goes down to 70 percent.

Before long, you're no longer communicating on a deep level. Your passion goes down to 60 percent. You can't resolve conflicts. Your passion goes down to 50 percent. You get weighed down by your jobs, taking care of your home, paying bills, the boring routine of life, and dealing with your families. Your passion goes down to 40 percent.

And then you do something that rocks your passion like a 9.0 earthquake: *you have a baby*. And just like that, he or she takes over your lives. You now live in a world of nonstop screaming, crying, pooping, spitting up, feeding, and all the other demands of this little person. Your passion drops to 0 percent.

If you have another baby, your passion may drop into negative territory.

As you're reading this, you're not shocked by this scenario, this erosion of passion, are you? It has already happened to you, or it's in the process of happening. You know how I know that? Because it happened to Sandy and me. Because it has happened to every couple I've ever met, somewhere between the fifth and fourteenth years of their marriage.

Okay, that's the bad news. The good news—really, the *great* news—is that you can get your passion back and keep it for the rest of your lives together. God has given us a how-to manual on passion. It's called the Song of Solomon. It was written by King Solomon of Israel, one of the greatest kings in history. Solomon and Shulamith, the two lovers in this amazing "song," show us how to create and maintain an outrageous, permanent passion.

WHY SHOULD WE LISTEN TO SOLOMON?

Wait, you may be thinking, *wasn't Solomon a womanizer?* Yes. Yes, he was. He ended up with seven hundred wives and three hundred concubines (1 Kings 11:3). So why should we listen to a man who was such a world-class womanizer? Why doesn't his awful, sinful behavior with women disqualify him from teaching us about passion? Fair questions. And I have four good answers.

First, I believe the Song of Solomon describes Solomon's first marriage, when he and Shulamith were totally focused on each other and doing everything right in their marriage. At this time in his life, Solomon was not involved with any other woman.

Second, late in his life, Solomon admitted his sexual sin and turned from it. In the book of Ecclesiastes, he clearly displays an attitude of humility and repentance. He has the guts to confess his sexual sin to the entire world and absolutely reject that sin.

Third, God placed the Song of Solomon in the Bible because He wanted us to learn valuable lessons from Solomon and Shulamith. Why else would this book be in the Bible? God chose to use these two spouses to teach couples how to love each other with a passionate love that will endure.

Fourth, the passion principles in the Song of Solomon work! They have worked in my marriage with Sandy. They have worked for thousands of couples I've seen in my therapy office and spoken to in my marriage seminars. As God does with all Christians, He has chosen to use a flawed person to communicate His truth.

So, enough about the legitimacy of Solomon's teaching. Let's move on.

COMMUNICATION: THE FOUNDATION OF PASSION

Passion starts with communication. Deep communication. The kind in which your hearts and minds are truly connecting. The kind in which you both are sharing personal things that you don't share with anyone else, issues that are deep in your hearts and often have to do with your view of yourself. Sharing feelings like that must involve opening yourselves up to the other. The trouble is, very few couples experience anything close to this level of communication. Why? Because God made the two sexes so incredibly different.

Picture the following scenario. (I think you'll recognize it.) A man and a woman are in conversation. It could be at home, in the car, or in a restaurant. Both are taking turns talking and listening. Then, suddenly, it happens. The woman notices that the man is not listening. She glances at him and sees the telltale signs: his mouth is hanging open, his eyes are glassy and staring off into the distance, and his body is as rigid as a statue.

It's not a stroke. It's not a seizure. It's not some kind of temporary paralysis. It's what all women hate. It's what drives them crazy. It's *the Zone.*

The Zone is a periodic mental blank spot that men move into without warning. In the Zone, there is little, if any, brain activity. For a brief period, conscious thoughts cease.

The woman takes the Zone personally and says, "You're not listening to me!" She's right. He's not. Now, it's bad enough at this point; the woman is insulted and angry because the man wasn't paying attention to her. But it gets worse. The woman, being a woman, has to ask this question: "What were you thinking about?" The man, being a man, with all sincerity, has to answer, "Nothing." The woman can't believe it. "What do you mean, *nothing*?" She can't conceive of going blank and having nothing on her mind. It has never happened to her. She's convinced he's lying. He had to be thinking of something!

Speaking on behalf of all men, ladies, let me assure you that the Zone is not an intentional attempt to drive you over the edge of sanity. It just seems that way. It's a perfectly natural part of being a man.

In fact, the Zone operates as a protective shutoff valve for a man's brain. When his brain is in danger of taking in too much information, it automatically shuts down. So, when your man zones out, you should be happy. *Wow, that was a close one. I guess I was talking too much.*

The Zone is just one difference between a man and a woman. There are a million differences! And all these differences block us in communication.

Solomon and Shulamith have the same differences all couples do. The wonderful thing is, they know how to get past all these differences and achieve a deep level of communication. The main way they do this is by "dancing the Four Step."

LET'S DO THE COMMUNICATION FOUR-STEP

God has designed a specific method couples can use to maneuver around their differences and connect—really connect—in conversation. I call this method the Communication Four-Step, and Solomon and Shulamith demonstrate it throughout the Song of Solomon. Each time these two lovers follow these four progressive steps, they develop intimate conversations. And what happens when you get intimate conversations? You get passion and plenty of it.

STEP ONE: WHEN YOU'RE APART, DWELL ON THE POSITIVE

The cycle of intimate communication begins *before* you ever sit down to talk. The method is simple: Whenever you're apart, fill your mind with positive thoughts about your partner. As you dwell on your sweetheart's wonderful qualities, your feelings of love will intensify. Your heart and your mind will open up. You will get excited about seeing your special person.

This first step occurs at the very beginning of the Song of Solomon. Shulamith is alone, and she is thinking very positive thoughts about Solomon. She loves his kisses (1:2), adores his lovemaking (1:2), is intoxicated by his scent (1:3), and believes everything about him has a beautiful fragrance (1:3).

Thinking these positive thoughts about her man sparks Shulamith's passion for Solomon and makes her want to be with him: "Draw me after you and let us run together! The king has brought me into his chambers" (1:4).

Chambers? What are they going to do in his chambers? Play checkers? Read the paper? Fold the laundry? No! They're going to talk on a deep level and then make love.

Remember back when you were dating and your love was blooming? You thought all kinds of positive things about your wonderful new partner all the time, didn't you? All those positive thoughts created intense feelings of love and longing to be with that amazing person, right?

Get back to doing this! It will reenergize your love and get you warmed up for your times of communication. When you dwell on the positive when you're apart, you'll be ready to open up when you get together to talk.

STEP TWO: MAKE TIME TO BE TOGETHER

Now that you're warmed up, you have to get together to talk.

To connect in conversation, you must have regularly scheduled times of communication. As I recommended in chapter 6, you need a minimum of four thirty-minute Couple Talk Times each week. No children present. No pets. No television, computer, or telephone. No distractions of any kind. Just the two of you in a private, quiet place in your home.

Who schedules these Couple Talk Times? The husband. Who makes sure they happen? The husband. Who leads in these talk times? The husband.

Solomon and Shulamith make time to be together throughout the Song of Solomon. One of the secrets to their incredible passion is their commitment to spend time together, away from everyone and everything else, on a regular basis.

I don't want to hear your lame excuses for why you can't meet with your spouse in four thirty-minute Couple Talk Times. It's not that you *can't*; it's that you *won't*.

Solomon was the king of Israel. A pretty busy guy, wouldn't you say? If Solomon could make time for Shulamith, you can make time for your spouse. We always make time for what's important to us.

Just this last week, I sat with a man and his wife in my therapy office. The man was so tied up with his career, his church, and his community organizations that he had no time left for his wife. I told him: "When you're divorced, you'll have plenty of time for your career, your church, and community organizations, but you won't have this wonderful woman to share your life with."

Make time every week to talk.

STEP THREE: WHEN YOU'RE TOGETHER, START WITH THE POSITIVE

You've warmed up for your time together by dwelling on your partner's positive qualities. Now you've sat down in a private, quiet place in your home to begin your thirty-minute Couple Talk Times. Now what do you do? Do what Solomon and Shulamith do: start by saying positive things about each other.

Every time Solomon and Shulamith are together—*every* time—they begin their conversation with special pet names and with praise. Right up front, they verbalize their love for one another. Their positive comments come before they bring up any topics. What they're doing is following up on the nonverbal positive thoughts they dwelt on when they were apart.

This burst of sweet positivity is the best way to start a Couple Talk Time. It automatically deepens Solomon's and Shulamith's level of conversation and helps them open up and share personally. It will do the same thing for you and your sweetheart.

Sandy Isn't Sandy, She's "Sweetie Carkst"

Solomon and Shulamith are into terms of endearment. Bigtime. Solomon calls Shulamith "my darling" nine times. Shulamith calls Solomon "my beloved" a whopping twenty-four times! Solomon also calls Shulamith "my dove" (Song of Solomon 2:14; 5:2; 6:9), "my bride" (Song of Solomon 4:8–12; 5:1), and "my perfect one" (5:2; 6:9). Shulamith calls Solomon "gazelle" or "young stag" (2:9, 17; 8:14), which means "stud" or "hunka-hunka burnin' love."

Taking my cue from Solomon, I call Sandy "Sweetie Carkst." "Carkst" is a form of Clarke. I also call her "Tweedie," a version of Sweetie, and "Special T." (I won't explain this one.) Silly? Sure. Sappy? You bet. Gushy? No question about it.

But do these cutesy names make Sandy feel special? Yes. Do they make her feel loved and closer to me? You bet. Do they create a positive flow and prepare her for a great conversation? No question about it.

Compliments Precede Conversation

After using pet names with each other, Solomon and Shulamith still aren't quite ready for dialogue. Just before they talk about whatever they're going to talk about, they lay some heavy-duty compliments on each other. They praise each other in two areas: physical beauty and character.

A good example of their mutual praise before deeper conversation is found in Song of Solomon 1:9–2:4. Here the compliments bounce back and forth between the lovers. It's as if they are trying to top each other with more and more flattering comments. As their praises flow, their passion intensifies and they become more and more vulnerable.

For starters, Solomon—using the imagery of his mare—tells Shulamith she is a beautiful and confident woman with excellent character (1:9–10). He lets her know that her cheeks and neck are stunning. He also calls her beautiful twice (1:15) and mentions the beauty of her eyes.

Shulamith responds by calling him "handsome" and "so pleasant" (1:16). She lets him know that he is very attractive physically and as a person.

Solomon fires back that she is "like a lily among the thorns" (2:2). This means she is the most beautiful and impressive woman he knows.

Shulamith responds by telling Solomon that he is "like an apple tree" in the forest (2:3). In other words, he protects her, and she feels safe with him.

Now, that's how you begin a loving, deep conversation! Does all this praise seem over-the-top to you? Does it make you feel uncomfortable? Believe me, you're not alone. Here's a dialogue I had recently with a husband after I urged his wife and him to begin their Couple Talk Times with mutual praise:

Husband:	All this praise between Solomon and Shulamith is overkill.
Dave:	No, it's not. It's what lovers do.
Husband:	But it's not real life! Couples don't do this kind of gushing praise. It's embarrassing.
Dave:	It is real love; that's what it is. This kind of mutual praise helped Solomon and Shulamith open up and talk personally. You know

	what's embarrassing? Sitting together with nothing to say.
Husband:	We did this praising thing back when we were dating. We've matured as a couple and moved past that stage.
Dave:	I'm sorry to hear that. You've lost something precious. Let me guess. You've also moved past your passion, haven't you? This mutual praise is not just for couples who are dating. It's for all couples, no matter how long they've been together. In fact, the longer you've been married, the more there is to praise.
Husband:	I'm just not a gushing, sweet, syrupy person.
Dave:	Then become one. You only have to be syrupy with one person on the face of the earth. Your wife. With practice, you'll get the hang of this praise thing. When your wife is happy and your conversations are deeper, you'll keep it up with—if not gush— gusto.

Start your Couple Talk Times the way Solomon and Shulamith start theirs: with pet names and with praise. I recommend you call your spouse one pet name, then say "I love you" and give her one compliment. The compliment can be for a physical attribute ("Your eyes are gorgeous"), a character trait ("I love that you are so affectionate"), or an action ("Thank you for making a wonderful meal last night").

You'll be amazed at how this opening burst of positivity deepens your conversations.

If you and your partner have endured a tough few days or you are in a painful place as a married couple, crank up the positives at the beginning of your Couple Talk Times. You need more positive flow to overcome the negativity in your relationship. Use two pet names and say "I love you" twice, and give two compliments. Neither of you may feel like doing this, but force yourselves to squeeze out these positives. It will make a difference in your conversations and in your feelings for each other.

STEP FOUR: TALK ABOUT EVERYTHING

I know it's hard to believe, but you're finally ready to talk. I still want you to use the Couple Talk Time stages I covered in chapter 6: create ambiance, pray a brief opening prayer, read your couples' devotional together, discuss any carryover topics, discuss current events, pray together, and move from prayer to conversation.

The final step in Solomon and Shulamith's Communication Four-Step—talk about everything—applies to the current events stage of your Couple Talk Times. The key here is being willing to bring up and discuss every possible topic. Virtually every topic in the known universe is fair game.

Too many couples place too many topics off-limits. They can't talk about sex. They can't talk about money. They can't talk about spiritual matters. They can't talk about in-law issues. They can't talk about _____ (fill in the blank).

Avoiding sensitive topics may help you not to fight, but it will also kill your passion. If you can't discuss areas of disagreement and pain, you can't resolve the underlying issues, and your resentments will grow year after year. The terrible weight of all these unresolved topics will crush the life from your relationship.

Eventually, these taboo topics will widen the gulf between you and your spouse, and before long you won't talk about anything significant. Silence, or sticking to superficial, safe topics, never produces passion.

Solomon and Shulamith have a wide-open, no-limits-allowed, we-can-talk-about-anything communication style. When they start talking in this fourth step, nothing is off the table. Check out this list of topics they discuss in the Song of Solomon:

> Her deepest insecurities. Her past traumas. Her lack of care for her body. Specific and detailed descriptions of each other's body parts. Friends. Family. Childhood. The need to refrain from premarital sex. Vacations they want to take. Conflicts between them. How to resolve a conflict. Misunderstandings. Specific and detailed descriptions of each other's personalities and character traits. Their feelings of love and passion for each other. What their bedroom looks like. Kissing. French kissing. Making out. Foreplay. Sexual intercourse. Detailed descriptions of their kissing, making out, foreplay, and intercourse. What they'd like to try in the bedroom. Having sex in the outdoors. Vacation sex. Exactly how she becomes lubricated prior to intercourse. The permanence of their love. The importance of keeping God at the center of their relationship. God being the source of their love. Their emotional connection. Their wedding day. The problem of indifference in marriage. Forgiveness.

See what I mean? Solomon and Shulamith are fearless when it comes to bringing up topics for conversation. They covered all these topics in only eight chapters! And this isn't even a complete list. Through Solomon and Shulamith, God is telling you and your spouse to have the freedom to talk about everything—from the most mundane and trivial to the most intimate and painful.

Don't ever say to your spouse, "I'm not going to talk about that." You have the right of refusal with just about any other person, but not with your spouse. To be a healthy and passionate couple, you *must* be willing to talk about *any* topic. You

may temporarily put off a conversation, but as soon as possible you need to go to your spouse and say, "I'm ready to talk about that now."

It's very common for one spouse to genuinely struggle to open up and share personally. It can be the husband. It can be the wife. If the strategies in this chapter don't lead to a breakthrough after two months, go *as a couple* to a Christian therapist. Work as a team on the problem. Together, with the right guidance, you will uncover and remove whatever is blocking the uncommunicative spouse from engaging in deep conversations—whether it's past, unresolved pain; personality issues; or marital issues.

If there are deep, unresolved wounds in your relationship, these wounds will hamper your ability (and probably your willingness) to communicate on a deep level. But you don't have to remain stuck there. Find a professional Christian therapist, and go through a process of healing. It will be painful, but along the way you can forgive and trust and learn to communicate on an intimate level.

1. On a scale of 1 to 10 (with 1 being outrageously dead and 10 being outrageously great), what is the level of passion each of you has toward the other?

    > Husband: 1 2 3 4 5 6 7 8 9 10
    > Wife: 1 2 3 4 5 6 7 8 9 10

    What has caused your passion to drop (or rise) to this level?

2. Read Song of Solomon 2:8–17 together, and see if you can identify the four steps of outrageous communication we discussed in this chapter.

3. How are you doing in your marriage when it comes to the Communication Four-Step? When you're apart, do you dwell on your spouse's positives? Are you scheduling and having four thirty-minute Couple Talk Times each week? At the beginning of your talk times, do you give mutual praise? Are you both willing to talk about everything?

4. What topics are off-limits when you talk? Why are these topics off-limits?

5. Agree, right now, that you will follow the Communication Four-Step in your Couple Talk Times this next week. Of course, first you must *schedule* four thirty-minute Couple Talk Times for the upcoming week.

10
"Baby, Don't Hurt Me"

I was going to begin this chapter with a funny story about sexual rejection in marriage. The only problem is, there's nothing even remotely funny about sexual rejection. Being turned down for sex by your spouse is one of the most painful experiences in marriage.

When you ask for sex, you are at your most vulnerable. If you get a *no*, you can't help but take it personally. It's not only a huge disappointment, it is also a stinging rejection. You are being denied satisfaction of a need that only your spouse can meet. And it's a powerful, core need—ranked right up there with hunger and thirst—that won't go away.

I'm not talking about the occasional forgoing of sex. I'm talking about a *pattern* of sexual rejection. When one spouse consistently says no to sex, the rejected spouse is deeply wounded. And the marriage is deeply wounded.

The rejected spouse feels angry, terribly frustrated, hurt, humiliated, and betrayed. Eventually, this spouse will stop asking for sex and will pull away from the rejecting partner. The rejected spouse will be much more susceptible to sexual sin: pornography, emotional affairs, physical affairs.

The rejecting spouse eventually becomes cold, unloving, and aloof, retreating behind a hard shell of defensiveness and apathy. In attempting to protect himself or herself, this spouse actually does great damage to himself or herself. By denying the other partner's sexual needs, the rejecting spouse also denies his or her own sexual needs.

Sexual rejection eviscerates a marriage. Respect, intimacy, passion, and love are stripped from the relationship. Without regular and healthy sex, a vital life-giving element in a marriage dies. It becomes a roommate relationship. A business relationship. A parenting relationship. You may stay together, but it will be a lackluster, low-grade, pathetic existence. You will live without the continual fun, excitement, and spontaneous thrills that God has designed uniquely for marriage and that can be found in nothing else.

As we'll see in chapters 11 and 12, God wants every married couple to enjoy frequent and vibrant times of physical and emotional intimacy. A passionate sex life is not an option for a married couple. It is a vital component of a great marriage. Without it, all you have is a piece of paper that says you're married.

I want to make it clear that sexual rejection goes both ways. A wife can reject her husband or a husband can reject his wife. In fact, in my experience as a psychologist—in my private practice and answering questions at my marriage seminars—just as many husbands reject their wives sexually as the other way around.

GOD IS AGAINST SEXUAL REJECTION

It's no accident that God addresses sexual rejection head-on in Song of Solomon. In fact, thirty-eight verses (5:2–7:10) are devoted to it. That's a big chunk of a small book!

In the New Testament, in a chapter dealing with marriage and sex, Paul writes:

> "Because of immoralities, each man is to have his own wife, and each woman is to have her own husband. . . . The wife does not have authority over her own body, but the husband does; and likewise also the husband does not have authority over his own body, but the wife does. *Stop depriving one another, except by agreement for a time, so that you may devote yourselves to prayer, and come together again so that Satan will not tempt you*" (1 Corinthians 7:2, 4–5, emphasis added).

Solomon and Shulamith show us how to apply Paul's teaching. These two biblical lovers do not allow sexual rejection to become an ongoing pattern in their marriage. Their actions teach us as couples how to avoid the devastating effects of rejection and enjoy a healthy sex life.

A Story as Old as Time

Get ready to read a sad story. A story you will find very familiar. A story that just about every married couple can instantly relate to. One spouse asks for sex and the other spouse says no. Ouch! Actually, much more pain is involved than a mere *ouch*.

Though the story is sad, it ends well. Very well.

From the Mountaintop to the Pits

It's interesting, and quite revealing, that this story of sexual rejection comes right after a peak sexual experience. Solomon and Shulamith have just made love for the first time (Song of Solomon 4:1–5:1), and it was marvelous. It is the first night of their honeymoon, and they are on top of the world.

Remember the first night of your honeymoon? The passion. The excitement. The thrill of seeing your soul mate naked. The incredible rush of pleasure and intimacy. The joy of sealing your love and commitment with intercourse. Wow! That was a night you'll never forget.

Suddenly, with a sickening thud, we are transported from sexual ecstasy to sexual misery. From wonderful sex to no sex. From mind-blowing intimacy to mind-numbing separation. With one little word, "no," Shulamith rocks her relationship with Solomon.

Despite the fact that at least some time has elapsed between the wedding night and this scene of sexual rejection, the placement of this story teaches an important truth: a loss of passion and sexual connection can happen at any time. Any married couple can go from great sex to lousy sex—or no sex—and it doesn't take long.

"Honey, Can We Make Love?" (5:2)

It's evening, and Solomon knocks on Shulamith's door. He is sexually aroused and asks her to open up so he can come in and make love to her. To communicate his love and attraction to her, he uses a string of endearments: "my sister, my darling, my dove, my perfect one!" (5:2). Solomon is making himself vulnerable, and he fully expects to get a yes.

"Not Tonight. I Can't Be Bothered" (5:3)

Shulamith says no to Solomon's sexual request and comes up with a lame excuse. She tells him she's already gotten ready for bed. Really? This is in the same category as "I have a headache" or "I'm too tired."

Saying no to sex is one thing. Saying "No, and I don't care" is much worse and painful. Shulamith stomps on Solomon's heart by telling him that staying in bed is more important than making love with him. It is her callous indifference that drives a stake into his heart.

Shulamith has allowed herself to become apathetic about sex with Solomon. She has gone from an engaged and responsive sexual partner to a disengaged and unresponsive sexual avoider. Sex with her husband is no longer a priority for her. That's sad, and it's wrong.

"You Hurt Me and I've Got to Get Away" (5:4–6)

Solomon, in one last attempt to be with her, tries the door, but it is locked. Wounded, he leaves. He doesn't just leave and go to another part of the house. He leaves their home to "get some space." Although he handles her rejection with loving maturity, he is hurt and feels betrayed.

"Oh No! What Have I Done?" (5:6–7)

It becomes clear to Shulamith how much she is hurting Solomon. She gets out of bed to let him in, but she is too late. He's gone. She realizes she is at fault and feels the weight of guilt. She's blown it!

Instead of getting back into bed, Shulamith immediately leaves the house and searches for Solomon. She calls out his name, but he does not answer. In a symbolic picture of the consequences of her rejection of Solomon, she is beaten by the night watchmen. The beating sends this message: apathy, and the sexual rejection it leads to, causes serious damage.

"My Husband Is the Best Man I Know" (5:10–16)

The beating doesn't stop her. Far from it. She accepts it as a reasonable consequence and continues to pursue Solomon. She goes on a run of praise for Solomon, complimenting his physical attractiveness and his outstanding character. Dwelling on his positives rekindles her passion for him.

"I Forgive You" (6:4–9)

She finally finds Solomon, and he graciously forgives her. In fact, he immediately goes on his own run of praise for Shulamith. He tells her she is the most beautiful woman in the world. She is unique. She is perfect. His words of tender, heartfelt praise reassure her of his great love for her.

"Let's Have Make-up Sex" (7:1–10)

To confirm their reconciliation and express their renewed commitment and love, Solomon and Shulamith make love. Their lovemaking is all the sweeter because of the difficult time they just went through. They have worked through the sexual rejection and are back on track as a couple.

The Solution for Sexual Rejection

God does not want your marriage to suffer from ongoing sexual rejection. When one spouse stops caring about sex, real damage is done to the relationship. The occasional no to sex is no big deal and won't kill a marriage. But a pattern of "No, I don't want sex" will undermine the marriage relationship.

In the sexual rejection scenario, there are two players: the rejecter and the rejected. As I mentioned before, the rejecter can be either the wife or the husband. Using the real-life example of Shulamith (the rejecter) and Solomon (the rejected), God provides specific instructions for each spouse in the "No,

I don't want sex" scenario.

First, here are the action steps for the *rejecter*.

OWN YOUR SEXUAL APATHY

Shulamith realizes that not caring about sex is wrong. It dawns on her that she has grown cold toward Solomon in the passion department. She embraces the brutal truth that her "I don't care" attitude about sex is her fault.

It just hits her, and it hits her hard. Suddenly, Shulamith is acutely aware that her avoidance of sex is way out of line. If you are guilty of a pattern of sexually rejecting your spouse, God wants it to hit you. Right now. And God wants you to do something about it.

Own your apathetic view of sex and resolve to take action to change.

FEEL YOUR PARTNER'S PAIN

Initially, Shulamith is quite comfortable with her rejection of her husband's sexual advances. She's fine with saying no. She feels perfectly justified in turning him away. To her, having gotten ready to go to bed is a solid reason to say no to sex. She doesn't feel even the slightest shred of guilt for locking Solomon out of the bedroom.

Sound familiar?

But once Solomon leaves her, her "Leave me alone" attitude evaporates. In an instant, she knows she has hurt her husband. Really and truly hurt him. Instead of being relieved at his departure, she is devastated. She feels real anguish.

She offers no excuses for her rejection of her husband. No attempts at justification. She finally "gets it." Solomon's walking away from their home makes her see that her ongoing rejection has wounded him severely. She feels bad because he is in such pain, and she feels even worse because she knows she has caused that pain.

Walk in your spouse's shoes and feel the pain of rejection. Admit that your lack of interest in sex is doing serious harm to your partner and to your marriage. And to you too. You are cheating yourself out of the joy of a regular, intimate sexual relationship.

Expose your reasons for avoiding sex for what they are: bogus excuses that drive a nail into your spouse's heart. Is taking care of your children more important than making love with your spouse? Is your career more important than making love with your spouse? Is cleaning your home more important than making love with your spouse? You know the answer to these questions.

If you continue to avoid making love with your mate, soon there will be no love left between you. You will force your spouse to deal with a high level of sexual temptation. You will push your spouse further and further away. At some point, your spouse will give up and stop asking for physical intimacy. When this happens—and it will—you will have succeeded in breaking your partner's heart.

PURSUE YOUR PARTNER

The moment Shulamith realizes how deeply she has harmed Solomon, she goes after him. She *immediately* leaves home and chases after him. Nothing is going to stop her from finding him. She runs out into the night, searching for her lover. She literally risks her life being out alone in the city at night. Not even a humiliating and painful beating from the night watchmen can stop her.

You, the rejecter, need to feel this same level of urgency. Now—*right now*—decide to go to your spouse and win back his or her heart. Get straight in your mind the three things you will say when you find your spouse. One, you will apologize for rejecting him or her sexually. Two, you'll let him or her know that you finally understand and feel the pain you have caused. Third, you will verbalize your love for him or her and will work together to get your sexual relationship back on track.

Focus on Your Partner's Positives

While Shulamith is looking for Solomon, she dwells on his many positive qualities. In a sudden burst of intense positivity (Song of Solomon 5:10–16), she lovingly describes his physical beauty and his impressive character. Why does she do this? To rekindle her passion for him!

Does her focusing on Solomon's positive traits actually work? You bet it does. Shulamith's passionate love and respect for Solomon come roaring back. At the end of her monologue of positivity, she wants him and she wants him bad. She once again desires him sexually.

It works for Shulamith, and it will work for you.

You need to rekindle your passion for your spouse. You've forgotten how great he or she is! If you tend to dwell on your spouse's negative qualities and weaknesses, stop doing that! Through Shulamith, God is telling you to stop being negative and apathetic.

Drop all the negatives, and stuff your mind and heart with all the positives you can think of. Remember how you felt about your spouse early in your relationship? Get those feelings back by dwelling on his or her sexy body and awesome character. To maintain your passion, continue to focus on your spouse's positive qualities as an attractive mate and as a *person*.

Your spouse is the most beautiful man or woman you know, and he or she is the best person you know. Right? Right!

Speak Truth to Your Spouse

Though the Song is silent on the matter, I have a pretty good idea of what Shulamith says to Solomon when she finds him. I think she communicates the three things I mentioned earlier: a heartfelt apology, empathy for the pain she has caused him, and her desire to be with him sexually. Because later they do make love (Song of Solomon 7:1–10), we know for sure that whatever she said to Solomon worked. Her passion for him got restarted, and so did her sexual desire for him.

I also think (though the Song doesn't report this either)

that Shulamith would have been honest with Solomon about all the issues affecting her sexual desire for him. If there were real, solid reasons for her sexual avoidance, I'm convinced she would have aired them with Solomon. We saw in the last chapter how this couple shared honest truth about every area of their individual lives and relationship.

So, in keeping with the Song's theme of total honesty, tell your spouse the specific reasons you have shied away from sex. It could be because of marital issues: how your spouse has treated you; not meeting your emotional and spiritual needs; lack of time together; an inability to work through conflicts; foreplay that doesn't last long enough to get you aroused and have an orgasm; affection after orgasm is not long enough or meaningful enough. . .

It could be your own unresolved personal issues: past abuse; neglect by your dad; poor self-image; pain transferred from previous romantic relationships; difficulty balancing responsibilities, such as kids, job, household chores; lack of energy because of everything else you do; lack of exercise and not eating right. . .

When you are honest with your spouse about what is causing you to avoid sex, the two of you can work together to resolve the issues. If you can't make progress on your own, get help from a licensed Christian therapist.

Now, let's take a look at the Song's action steps for the *rejected*. His or her responsibilities are not as extensive, but they are nonetheless important.

Be Gracious When Rejected

Responding to rejection with grace is easier said than done. I know. In fact, it is incredibly difficult. But it's what Solomon does. When Shulamith refuses his request for sex, Solomon is probably angry. Certainly, he's hurt. He could have yelled at Shulamith. He could have pounded the bedroom door in frustration. He could have said some mean, nasty things to her to vent his pain.

Solomon does none of these things. What does he do instead? Nothing. Nothing at all. He simply leaves without saying a word to Shulamith. Wow! That takes courage and impressive self-control. Psychologically, it is a brilliant move. He doesn't make *his response to her rejection* the issue. He makes *her rejection of him* the issue.

When Solomon graciously and quietly leaves, Shulamith's heart is touched. She feels bad about rejecting her loving husband for no good reason. Her feelings of love for him are stirred, and she goes after him.

Husband, if you ask for sex and are rejected—whether it's an occasional rejection or a pattern of rejection—follow Solomon's example and quietly pull back. This prevents you from sinning with your response and has the best chance of motivating your wife to pursue you.

You could vent your anger and frustration with her. You could slam some cabinets and doors. You could attack her lame excuses. You could get back at her with some passive-aggressive behavior, such as not doing certain household chores. But these responses would only lead to her being defensive and feeling justified in rejecting you. She'd think: *He's so mean, and that's why I don't want to sleep with him.*

If you go with the kind and gentle approach, you'll give her no reason to be annoyed and defensive. Let her know you want to be with her sexually but that you'll wait until she's ready. Ask her to let you know when she's ready to make love. Then drop the subject and walk away.

With this approach, there's at least a chance she'll think, *I hurt him badly. I rejected him, and my reason is weak. Why did I do that? I do love him.*

Stay Away from Sexual Sin

In my professional opinion, sexual rejection is a key factor in our culture's obscenely high rate of sexual addiction, adultery, and divorce. Satan uses sexual rejection as a wedge to destroy thousands of spouses and marriages.

Satan's malevolent wisdom can convince people that sexual rejection legitimizes extramarital sex. The Bible teaches that extramarital sex is *sin* and *contrary to God's will* (1 Thessalonians 4:3; Hebrews 13:4). Because of this, it can destroy a marriage. In Solomon's other writings, he instructs husbands to "drink water from your own cistern" (Proverbs 5:15); that is, find your sexual satisfaction with your wife; and "rejoice in the wife of your youth. . .let her breasts satisfy you at all times; be exhilarated always with her love" (Proverbs 5:18–19).

If your spouse regularly rejects you sexually, it will intensify the temptation to seek sexual satisfaction outside of your marriage. You may be tempted to use pornography. You may be tempted to go to a strip club. You may be tempted to begin an adulterous relationship. Any sexual activity outside of your marriage is sin. It brings dishonor to the Lord who loves you and died for you to forgive your sins, and it grieves His Spirit (Ephesians 4:30). And it will do great damage to you, your spouse, your marriage, and your children. You don't get a "pass" just because your spouse has rejected you in the bedroom.

To stay pure, stay close to God. Maintain a daily quiet time with God, praying and reading the Bible. Stay in a local church and serve in that church. Stay in an accountability relationship with another person of the same sex, meeting face-to-face at least once a week.

BE GRACIOUS WHEN YOUR SPOUSE IS READY

When your spouse comes to you with an apology and a desire to be with you sexually, be gracious and kind. That's how Solomon reacts when Shulamith comes to him. He doesn't use sarcasm. He doesn't vent anger and resentment. He doesn't make it hard on her at all. There is no payback for her rejection of him.

As soon as Shulamith finds him, Solomon launches into a string of wonderful compliments (Song of Solomon 6:4–9). He praises her physical attractiveness and her uniqueness as a woman. He makes it clear he does not want to be with any other woman. During their conflict, he has remained faithful to her.

Solomon's praise of Shulamith assures her of his complete forgiveness and his deep love for her. Also, he is reconnecting with her on an emotional level. He knows that emotional connection must come before physical connection.

When your spouse comes to you to reconcile and get back on track sexually, do what Solomon did. Forgive quickly, and let her know you still love her as much as ever. In order to forgive her, you may need to talk about the pain her rejection has caused. But do this as quickly as possible and in a loving way.

HAVE MAKE-UP SEX

Make-up sex is some of the sweetest, most intimate sex you can experience. Solomon and Shulamith are the poster couple for make-up sex. Once Solomon forgives Shulamith for rejecting him and assures her of his love for her, they seal their reconciliation by making love.

When you haven't been together physically because of sexual rejection, you need to get back into the bedroom as soon as possible. Once you make up emotionally, you need to make up physically.

If you've been out of practice for a while, it's okay to go slow. Kiss, make out, massage, and do foreplay without intercourse. After a few days, maybe a week or so, you'll be warmed up and ready for the entire sexual experience.

Your renewed lovemaking completes your healing from sexual rejection and confirms the rekindling of your passion for each other.

Outrageous Interaction

1. Talk to each other about sexual rejection in your
   marriage. Is it an occasional issue, or has it become
   a pattern?
2. If you are the *rejecter,* share your reasons with your
   spouse. Be willing to admit, if needed, that some of
   your reasons are just excuses. Talk about any reasons
   that you feel are serious and legitimate for *why* you
   avoid sex. Dig deeper, and share honestly.
3. If you are the *rejected,* share your pain with your
   spouse. Honestly and lovingly express what it's been
   like to be rejected. Tell your spouse why you think he
   or she has been avoiding sex. Talk about your own
   behaviors that may precipitate rejection and about
   issues you see in your spouse's life that elicit rejection.
4. Agree that together you will follow the solution for
   sexual rejection described in this chapter. First, the
   rejecter will do his or her steps, and then the rejected
   will do his or her steps.

11
"Baby, Get Me Ready for Great Sex"

The sex life of the black widow spider and her mate is very simple and straightforward. Acting on instinct, the spiders have sex. The act is brief and easily accomplished. Immediately following sex, the black widow kills and eats her mate. Hence, the name "black *widow*." Very neat. Very clean. Very easy.

Some ladies may feel like killing and eating their husbands after sex. I know it's tempting, but I'm not recommending that. That's not my point.

My point is that I envy these spiders because sex is so easy for them. It's too bad the guy has to die, but it's easy. At least he died with a smile on his face. The sex life of humans is not nearly as simple and straightforward. In fact, sex can be—and usually is—one of the most awkward and confusing parts of marriage.

Here's the bad news: many obstacles stand between you and joyful, passionate sex. But here's the good news: with the right information, hard work, and God's help, listening to Him and trusting Him, you can build a tremendous sex life. That's what God desires for every married couple.

What you need, dear reader, is an expert with the wisdom and courage to present a clear, practical plan to produce some serious passion in your sex life. That expert couldn't be convinced to write this chapter Himself. But He asked me to do my best.

Rest assured, I'm not going to share Dave Clarke's wisdom on sex. That wouldn't take us very far. Just ask Sandy. I'm going to share God's wisdom on sex. God has given us a sexual instruction book for married couples. It's called the Song of Solomon.

The Song tells us what to do *before the bedroom* to prepare for great sex. The Song also tells us what to do *in the bedroom* to experience great sex.

This chapter will focus on what happens *before* the bedroom. Chapter 12 will focus on what happens *in* the bedroom.

In addition to all our other differences, men and women have major sexual differences. We prepare for great sex by understanding our sexual differences and finding solutions for them. Let's take a look at these differences and the solutions offered by the Song of Solomon.

AROUSAL AND EMOTIONAL STATE

For the man, arousal is not directly connected to his emotional state. Circumstances mean nothing to him After a long, stressful day, most men are still likely to want sex. Sex can be a way to release his stress.

Ten minutes after an argument with his wife, he'll say, "Hey, honey, how about you and me?" The woman is horrified! She can't believe he's serious. The argument and strained feelings are still fresh—not even resolved—and he wants sex? She thinks, *What's the matter with him?* He's a man, that's what's wrong with him.

A hurricane is sweeping across the house. Nuclear missiles are inbound. An earthquake is shaking the foundation of the home. None of these make any difference to the man if he wants sex. "Honey, the missiles won't hit for another ten minutes. We can do it! What a way to go out, huh?"

His dear wife is in bed, sick as a dog. She has a thermometer in her mouth, VapoRub smeared on her chest, and a pile of used tissues all around her. Her husband sits down next to her on the bed. She expects to hear an expression of sympathy and support. Instead, she hears, "The kids are watching a video. Let's have sex. We won't kiss, because I don't want to catch what you have. I think sex will take your mind off your pain."

She is sound asleep in the middle of the night. But she's not safe from his sexual urges. She is awakened by his groping hands and these words: "Honey, are you asleep?" She'd like to reply, "No, I was lying awake at 2:00 a.m. hoping you'd want sex. You made my dream come true!"

For the woman, arousal is directly connected to her emotional state. Circumstances mean everything to her. How she feels personally and how she feels in the relationship will determine how she feels about sex.

If she's not happy and satisfied with herself or the relationship, she's a brick wall, sexually speaking. She cannot respond sexually. How her day has gone and how her man has treated her will determine her level of interest in sex.

If she's had a bad day and something happened that is bothering her, she has to talk it out with her husband before sex is an option. If an issue is unresolved between her and her husband, they must work it out before she can even consider sex.

If she doesn't feel that her man loves and cares for her and listens to her, sex will be repulsive to her. Or it may feel like just another chore: make dinner, feed the dog, change the kitty litter, have sex with Bob. Without a feeling of closeness and security with her man, her response to sex—if she even agrees to it—will be: "Well, all right, if you have to have it! Go ahead and get it over with!"

THE SONG'S SOLUTION

In Song of Solomon 2:14, we are given a glimpse of a Couple Talk Time between Solomon and Shulamith:

> "O my dove, in the clefts of the rock,
> In the secret place of the steep pathway,
> Let me see your form,
> Let me hear your voice;
> For your voice is sweet,
> And your form is lovely."

This is Solomon speaking to Shulamith. They're alone in a private, quiet place. There are no distractions. They're going to have a conversation. Solomon wants to hear her talk. He's not even touching her at all. The touching will come later. He's going to *listen* to her. . .really listen to her.

EMOTIONAL CONNECTION MUST COME FIRST

These two lovers know that emotional connection must precede physical connection. Not only do they meet in a private place to talk, but they also know *how* to talk to achieve depth in conversation (see the discussion in chapter 9 about the Communication Four-Step).

Solomon and Shulamith always connect emotionally in conversation before they make love. *Always.* This is the Song of Solomon's first solution to your differences in the area of arousal and emotional state.

Before intercourse, make sure to have a time of communication and connection. It doesn't have to be long, but you *must talk.* As you talk in a private place in your home, you each clean out the day's stresses and reconnect as a couple.

When you reconnect, you're ready for sex.

Both the man and the woman need this reconnection. Every couple gets disconnected over the course of a day and must come back together. First comes the emotional rebonding. Then the physical reunion can follow.

Husband, you can't just grab your wife and have sex. I wish you could—I wish *I* could with Sandy—but it's not possible. This kind of immediate, "no need for any emotional connection" sex may happen on the honeymoon and then never again! Let's have a moment of silence for our honeymoon sex. . .because it's over.

And, it's a good thing it's over. With the right preparation, your sex will be five hundred times better than your honeymoon sex.

KISS LIKE YOU MEAN IT

Second, the Song of Solomon teaches lovers to engage in regular kissing sessions as part of the preparation for making love. Too many couples kiss intensely only when they are in foreplay. Solomon and Shulamith show us that deep kissing in the hours and days leading up to intercourse greatly enhances the lovemaking experience.

Solomon and Shulamith know it's important to kiss often. They know it's important to deliver quality, meaningful, "I'm in love with you" kisses. And that's exactly what they do throughout the Song. There isn't one dud kiss in the entire Song of Solomon!

"How beautiful is your love, my sister, my bride! How much better is your love than wine" (4:10).

Solomon says that Shulamith tastes better than wine. He could say this only because he's done his research. He has tasted her ruby red lips with some heavy-duty kisses!

Read this next verse, and tell me what kind of kiss is going on:

"Your lips, my bride, drip honey; honey and milk are under your tongue" (4:11).

It's French kissing, right here in the Bible! Sexy! Sensuous! Erotic! Passionate! These two lovers are swapping oral bacteria and loving it.

Shulamith weighs in on their kissing with this brazen, "I want your lips," line:

"His lips are lilies dripping with liquid myrrh" (5:13).

She says she loves Solomon's wet kisses. She knows that every great kiss involves generous amounts of saliva.

Stop giving each other lame, wimpy, pathetic kisses. No more tiny pecks. No more cheek kisses. No more bone-dry, closed-mouth kisses. Are you kissing your mother or Uncle Bob? Stop it! Your kisses are supposed to generate passion, not suck it out of your marriage.

I know you know how to really kiss each other. You used to do it all the time. Bring back real kissing, and bring it back today. Every kiss, no matter where or when it occurs, ought to be a full-bore, gum-scorching, lingering, heartfelt smacker! Sucky face, that's what I'm talking about.

And, by the way, is one kiss—even if it's a real lulu—going

to be enough? No! You can't get enough of your sweetheart's lips! Two or three massive mouth bangers are a must.

When you part in the morning, lay some juicy kisses on each other. Do the same when you come back together at the end of the day. All during the week, the days and hours when you're home, kiss like you mean it: before and after your Couple Talk Times, when you first wake up, in the kitchen, during a television show, when you go to bed. . . You get the idea.

I've had men complain to me, "But, Dave, if I kiss my wife like this when I'm leaving for work, I'll be all sexually excited and I won't be able to do anything about it!"

I respond, "Sexual excitement with your wife is a good thing. When you get home later that day, you can do something about it."

It's like those silly television commercials for male virility drugs. In a very serious voice, the announcer warns: "If your erection lasts more than four hours, call your doctor." I say, "Why? To say thank you?" An erection that occurs because you've planted some powerful kisses on your beautiful wife is a very good thing.

WIFE, GET YOURSELF IN THE MOOD

Shulamith becomes sexually aroused because Solomon connects with her emotionally prior to any physical touching. Shulamith becomes sexually aroused because she and Solomon have a fully developed kissing life. Shulamith also becomes sexually aroused because she works at getting herself in the mood for making love.

Shulamith gets herself aroused at the very beginning of the book! She is alone and thinking of her physical relationship with her man:

> *"May he kiss me with the kisses of his mouth! For your love is better than wine" (Song of Solomon 1:2).*

> *"Draw me after you and let us run together! The king has brought me into his chambers" (Song of Solomon 1:4).*

Shulamith is picturing all the passionate kisses Solomon is going to plant on her luscious lips. She is looking forward to Solomon taking her to his bedroom and making love to her. She is getting in the mood, and Solomon isn't even around!

In Song of Solomon 5:10–15, right in the middle of their unresolved conflict, Shulamith dwells on Solomon's beautiful body and wonderful character traits. Again, she's not with Solomon at the time.

- She says he is handsome. Dazzling, even. She describes his character as outstanding.
- She loves his eyes because they are soft and express his love for her.
- She is amazed by his cheeks. These are the cheeks on his face, by the way. (Although I bet she likes his other cheeks too.)
- She says his lips give her gentle, sweet, and lubricated kisses.
- She believes he has abs of ivory! His abs look great and display his strength.
- She loves his powerful body and the fact that he is stable in troubled times.
- She thinks he is distinguished and regal as a person. He has great dignity.

Do you get what Shulamith is doing here? She is fantasizing about her husband. She is focusing on how marvelous he is—as a physical specimen and as a man. She is getting more and more aroused as she fantasizes. In a very healthy and God-honoring way, she is preparing to be with her husband sexually.

Husbands don't need instruction on fantasizing about being with their wives. We do it all the time. It comes naturally. Wives need to work at it.

Wife, do what Shulamith does. Most wives hardly ever—if at all—get themselves aroused by dwelling on the physical characteristics and character traits of their husbands. Shulamith not only does it, but she goes on and on as she creates an incredibly positive picture of the man she loves.

Take time each day—at least five to ten minutes—and think hard about your husband's positives. Center your thoughts on your stud's most impressive physical parts and his character qualities. What happens to Shulamith will happen to you: a growing sexual arousal directly connected to your man.

How Arousal Happens

A man is aroused primarily by what he sees. It's visual. For a man, looking at his wife's body gets him excited. When she takes off her clothes, his arousal is immediately triggered. His motto is, "All I need is my wife and a mattress."

A woman is aroused by words, touch, atmosphere, lighting, mood, and context. Husband, you may be thinking, *What do you mean by* context? Context is all the things that make up the experience.

Women notice the details and are affected by them. They notice every part of the lovemaking environment. They miss nothing. Husband, let me tell you something you're not going to like: Just seeing your naked body isn't enough for your wife. I know that's a shock. In fact, your naked body might be the problem. (Just kidding.)

The Song's Solution

Solomon and Shulamith make love by lamplight in a beautiful setting. Shulamith comments on the beauty of their bedroom (Song of Solomon 1:17). She says to Solomon: "I like it in here!" So, take a hint and do what they do.

Make Your Bedroom a Love Nest

I recommend you work together to make your bedroom a soft, warm, romantic place prior to intercourse. In other words, make it a love nest. Make the bed. Close the closet doors. Clean up the clutter. You want to focus on the bed, don't you?

Put on some soft music. Make sure the room has low, soft light. Light a few candles for a very special light. You don't want it pitch dark or too bright. Everybody looks better in low light.

Caveman, get rid of your pile of dirty clothes. You know you have one (pile) somewhere in your bedroom. Your wife will see the pile, and it'll bother her. She'll feel as if she's making love to a pile of dirty clothes.

Your bedroom ought to be the most beautiful, spectacular room in your home. Husband, if she wants a new mattress, buy it. A dresser? Buy it. A new lamp, new wallpaper, new flooring—buy it all! If you're thinking, *Dave, you're killing me! This will cost me a fortune!* my response is, "Yes, it will. But what will you get in return? A happy, more sensuous wife. And better sex."

Husband, you could make love in the garage. The environment makes little difference to you. The place of lovemaking makes a huge difference to your wife. So, open your wallet and spruce up that bedroom.

What You Wear Is Important

Husband, don't ever come to bed in your raggedy underwear and twenty-year-old stained T-shirt. This ruins the context! She won't be impressed. Play it safe and smart and ask her what to wear to bed. Red big-boy briefs. Superman Speedo. Nothing. No one will know, and whatever you wear, it's coming off anyway, right?

Wife, wear sexy lingerie and nighties. Please. Solomon writes in Song of Solomon 4 that Shulamith wore a perfumed, see-through negligee. Let's just say it's a big hit with Solomon.

Wife, I think I speak for your husband when I suggest you get rid of the winter flannel nightgown. It's like going to bed with a pup tent. I've know men who have suffocated in the folds of a flannel nightgown. Some died of a broken heart because they couldn't find a body in that big old tent.

He wants to see your body. Is that a crime?

The Speed of Arousal

For the man, arousal happens quickly. Orgasm can literally be in seconds. The man thinks, *I've got my erection, let's go! I can have my orgasm right now, so what are we waiting for?* There is no buildup to arousal. It's just there. Boom!

For the woman, arousal happens more slowly. It takes time. Orgasm cannot happen right away. A slow, steady buildup leads to arousal and orgasm. The woman thinks, *What's the rush? Are we catching a plane in ten minutes?* The woman is not impressed with the man's quick orgasm. She won't hold a stopwatch and say, "Wow! Five minutes flat! Way to go, honey! I don't know how you do it!"

On average, a woman takes thirty minutes from the beginning of foreplay to complete arousal. Thirty minutes! More if she has been stressed or preoccupied and needs extra time to relax and respond sexually.

The Song's Solution

In the Song, Solomon and Shulamith take their time in foreplay. For them, it's a slow, gradual progression toward intercourse. Soft, loving words and gentle touches lead to greater and greater arousal.

Let's say both husband and wife could orgasm in a minute and a half. That would be too fast! You need more time to express, verbally and physically, your love for each other in the bedroom. That's why God made the woman to need more time to be aroused.

Solomon and Shulamith demonstrate their slow, patient foreplay in chapter 4 of the Song. By taking time, the two lovers reach higher and higher levels of arousal. And who leads this slow, gradual process of foreplay? Solomon!

Husband, Slow Down!

Husband, your erection is certainly a tremendous event and very impressive. It's probably the highlight of your day. But it doesn't mean your orgasm should happen right away.

Give your woman more time—in fact, *as much time as she needs* to be aroused. This may be difficult for you, but it will pay off. She will be more responsive, and making love to a wife who is excited about what's going on is a whole lot more fun. She'll be able to achieve orgasm, which pleases her and you.

Do you ever wonder why your wife isn't into sex and doesn't seem to enjoy it? Chances are, you're too fast, and she's not aroused yet. If intercourse happens before she is sufficiently lubricated, it will be painful for her—which is exactly what you *do not want*, especially for her.

Husband, your orgasm will be more intense if you wait. The longer you can wait, the better it will be.

Keep in mind, husband, that the thirty minutes your wife needs to get ready should never be tedious. It should not be drudgery for you. You're not waiting, sitting on the edge of the bed: "Are you ready? It's been twenty-eight minutes." No! You're touching her, caressing her, kissing her. You're loving her. It's fun—the best kind of fun—getting her ready. Foreplay is fun!

SPECIFIC DIFFERENCES BETWEEN COUPLES

Each married couple has unique differences. Discussing these differences and reaching understanding and compromises *before* the bedroom is critically important. Consider these four main areas:

Who. Who initiates sex in your relationship? Talk about it, and decide which partner will ask for sex: one person each time or either?

How. How is the initiating done? How do you like to ask or be asked? Let's say the husband's typical approach is to clap his hands together, whisper in his wife's ear, "Hey, sweetie, you and me," and then utter two grunts. If the wife isn't wild about this approach, she must tell him what would work better for her. Maybe the husband wants his wife to use these words: "Hey, baby, I want to make love to you tonight. What do you want me to wear?" Because the husband is probably thinking sex and his wife is not, often it's best for the husband to ask if the next evening (or morning or whatever) will be okay with her. This takes into consideration how the wife is feeling, how she can fit it into her plans.

When. How often will you have intercourse? All couples differ here. That is a decision—a plan—each couple must discuss and choose. There is no set number. (No, wait! A number is forming in my mind. Four! Four times a week! No, not really.)

The nymphomaniac craves sex every day. The refrigerator wants sex only once every six months. Although couples usually don't have to face such a wide disparity in desire, it's important to talk about it and cut a deal, one that fully considers the needs of both. If the one spouse wants sex four times a week and the other prefers just once a week, how about trying twice a week? Work at it, and you'll find a number that fits your relationship and is acceptable to both spouses. But whatever you decide, it's an issue that must be addressed and resolved, and not just left in confusion.

What. What is pleasurable for each partner during foreplay and intercourse? What kind of touching? What positions do you want to try? Be specific. "I like _____. I don't like _____." Keeping your desires and dislikes a secret ensures that your spouse won't meet your sexual needs. Practice makes perfect. The more lovingly you engage in sex, experimenting, asking questions of one another, the sooner you will discover what gives your spouse pleasure. And then you will have hit the jackpot.

Talk about what is blocking you from really enjoying sex. Husbands and wives both get blocked, and the reasons are most often very different, gender-specific, unknown to the other. All couples have sexual problems at times. Talk about these areas before you get into the bedroom. The conversation may be awkward and difficult, but it will pay off.

You're almost ready for intercourse. When you work through the Outrageous Interaction steps for this chapter, you both will better understand three vital areas: your basic sexual differences, the Song's solutions to the problems resulting from these differences, and the four categories above (*who, how, when,* and *what*). With these discussions under your belt, you will be prepared to get deeper and more personal as you move into the bedroom.

Outrageous Interaction

1. Commit right now, both of you, to have a time of communication and reconnection before every sexual interaction.
2. Evaluate the state of your kissing life. What changes do you need to make to get your smackers back on track?
3. Wife, what obstacles get in the way of your getting in the mood for making love? Are you willing to follow Shulamith's example in becoming aroused prior to intercourse?
4. Husband and wife, what can you do to make your bedroom into a love nest prior to intercourse? Tell your spouse what clothing you prefer him or her to wear.
5. Wife, do you need more time to become aroused in foreplay? Tell your husband how much time you think you need. Tell him what pleases you and arouses you most. Husband, tell your wife what pleases you and arouses you most.
6. Talk about your specific differences and preferences: *who, how, when, what.*

12
"Baby, Make Love to Me"

In chapter 9, you learned how to reach deep levels of emotional connection in your conversations. In chapter 10, you learned how to deal with the potentially devastating impact of sexual rejection. In chapter 11, you learned how to prepare for physical intimacy by understanding your sexual differences and finding solutions to any difficulties that arise from these differences. Keep in mind that differences are good, sometimes wonderful, and never bad.

Armed with these foundational principles from the Song of Solomon, you are now ready to discover what the Song says about the act of making love. I can sense your excitement. That's right. . .you are ready to enter the bedroom.

Here are Solomon's instructions for your periods of sexual activity.

BE AS CLEAN AND ATTRACTIVE AS POSSIBLE

Solomon and Shulamith prepare their bodies for sex. They use perfumed oils (Song of Solomon 1:3) and fragrance (4:11). They don't just dive into bed. They get their bodies ready.

Take a shower before you make love. Come to think of it, take a shower *together*. You might never get to the bed. Husband, this could start the thirty minutes of foreplay. By the time you get to bed, you'll have only twenty minutes to go before the big event. Do not—ever—think that foreplay is not an integral part of the big event, because it is. Too many husbands think mainly or mostly of the "main event." This is a gigantic mistake, especially with regard to the woman's pleasure.

You can, on occasion, make love in the shower. It's not against the law. (I checked.) But only if it's a mutual desire. With all the soap and water running, there is no cleanup afterward.

Use deodorant, perfume, or cologne if this pleases your spouse. I hate to be the one to tell you this, but your body doesn't smell good on its own. Ever bury your face in a sweaty armpit? Oh, that's fun!

Brush your teeth, and use a little mouthwash. If you've just eaten a bag of sour cream and onion potato chips, who wants to kiss you? Even the dog would turn away.

Husband, you have to shave. If you don't, for her it's like being scraped by sandpaper. Maybe your wife likes it rough: "Scrape me, baby, scrape me!" But really, I doubt if she'll enjoy your stubble. Her skin is soft and delicate, and your bristles will irritate it.

There is one exception to this shaving instruction. If you have a mustache or a beard and your wife likes it, that's fine. Just keep it groomed. Keep food out of it. If she doesn't like your facial hair, you have trouble. You'll have to shave it off or wear some kind of plastic mask.

Focus on Pleasing Your Partner and Yourself

Solomon and Shulamith talk quite a bit during sex. Why? To make sure their needs will be met. When you're in bed together, communicate to your partner what makes you feel good. Your partner cannot meet your sexual needs unless you make them clear. Tell your spouse what you like. This isn't selfish, it's practical.

Do what Solomon and Shulamith do in chapters 4 and 7 in the Song: Focus on one person at a time. Going one at a time, for foreplay and orgasm, makes sure both of you get what you need. When it's your partner's turn, you are a sex slave and will do whatever pleases him or her, with the exception, of course, of those sexual behaviors that the two of you have already agreed are off limits.

Husband, here's a suggestion: Let your wife go first most of the time. In Solomon and Shulamith's two main sexual encounters in the Song (chapters 4 and 7), Shulamith goes first. This makes sense for two reasons. One, a good husband is a sacrificial servant and puts his wife's needs above his own. Second, because it takes the woman longer to be aroused, choosing to postpone his own pleasure keeps the husband engaged and focused.

Use nonverbal communication to tell your partner that something feels bad or painful. It's easy to get pretzeled up in bed: a knee in the groin, fingernails digging into skin, the woman's long hair whipping across her husband's face, lack of vaginal lubrication. Shouting "Stop that, it hurts!" typically kills the mood. So try agreed-upon signals, such as a touch on the shoulder or gently moving a hand to a different body part.

SPEND TIME IN FOREPLAY

Without foreplay, the sex act itself is boring. Extended foreplay is loads of fun and an essential part of the anticipation and preparation for orgasm. Caressing, touching, kissing, massaging, fondling, and talking are all important. Well, not too much talking. Husband, if you've talked to her before the bedroom, she won't have to talk as much during foreplay. In bed, you only want to talk about your lovemaking, right?

The husband can easily focus only on orgasm—his own orgasm, that is. "I mean, isn't my ejaculation the point of this exercise? Foreplay lasts only until I'm ready to do my thing, right?" Wrong! Foreplay should last twenty-five to thirty minutes, or until both partners are sufficiently aroused and ready for orgasm.

In the previous chapter, I wrote about the importance of extending foreplay. Solomon and Shulamith take their sweet time in foreplay. For them, it is a beautiful, slow, gradual process. Now, let's concentrate on chapters 4 and 7 in the Song and find out exactly what these two lovers do in their foreplay.

- Solomon praises Shulamith's physical and emotional beauty. He compliments the lovely parts of her body, and her character. He starts at her head and slowly moves down her body. His tender and heartfelt praise has three results: It builds her confidence in her beauty; it confirms that he loves all of her and not just her body; and it arouses both of them (4:1–7). Solomon tells Shulamith he is prepared to make love to her all night long. This man is not in a hurry!

- He tells her how much she arouses him (4:9).
- He praises her lovemaking and her sensual kisses (4:10–11).
- He describes her lovely body and how he's intoxicated by it (4:13–14).
- He acknowledges that she is sexually aroused (4:15).
- She speaks and indicates she's ready for intercourse. She knows there is no way Solomon can know when she is sufficiently aroused and is ready for him to enter her if she doesn't tell him. So she tells him (4:16).

In chapter 7, the lovers follow a similar pattern.

- Solomon again begins foreplay with praise of Shulamith's physical beauty and her excellent character. This time he starts at her feet and moves slowly up her body (vv. 1–7).
- He touches and kisses her breasts and enthusiastically describes her erotic, deep kisses (vv. 8–9).

Husband, if you're too fast, three things happen, and they're all bad. One, your wife won't become aroused. Two, she won't have an orgasm. Three, she'll feel as if the whole sexual experience is all about you, which is just what you *don't* want her to think or feel.

But if you take your time in foreplay, as Solomon does, just the opposite happens. First, she can become aroused. Second, she can have an orgasm. Third, she'll feel that the whole sexual experience is about both of you.

Healthy foreplay is extremely enjoyable. It helps you practice pleasing your partner. It is a wonderful way, in all of marriage, a *unique* way, of expressing your love. And it leads to a more intense orgasm for both husband and wife.

The husband might be afraid of losing his erection if he waits. If you extend foreplay, you *will* lose your erection. But you'll get it back. The erection comes and goes during foreplay. Don't panic. Don't look down and yell, "It's gone! It'll never come back!" It will come back when you need it.

Let me make one more important point here. Simultaneous orgasm is largely a myth. It is possible, and it does happen, but only very seldom. It happens all the time on television shows and in the movies, but that's make-believe. And you shouldn't be watching that stuff anyway.

Most women achieve orgasm as the man manually and gently stimulates the clitoris. This, the wife's orgasm, can happen before or after intercourse, and before or after the man's orgasm.

Wife, just for fun, try this approach. Have your husband bring you to orgasm first. Then say, "Thanks, honey, that was great! Well, gotta go!" Hop out of bed and leave the room. This will be payback for all the times he's had his orgasm and left you unsatisfied. Actually, I'm kidding. Revenge is wrong and petty. The goal is for both of you to achieve orgasm.

BE PLAYFUL IN BED

Sex, at its most basic level, is play. (Of course, God gave sex for procreation, which is sacred and wonderful. But aside from conception, all the other thousands of times a couple has sex, the purpose is pleasure, bonding, a special way of expressing love, unifying. . . . So, it is not and never should be a duty, or a reward.) Good old-fashioned, free, creative, and spontaneous play. I talk to too many couples who aren't having much sexual fun. Sex is not a deadly serious drama. It is a romantic comedy.

Solomon and Shulamith act like a couple of kids in bed. This playfulness is part of the secret of their exciting sex and—for all couples—always will be.

Stop having sex the same tired way time after time.

Early in their marriage, most couples find one way that works. A foreplay routine and a position that gets the job done. Orgasms are achieved. And that's fine for a while. But by the three hundredth time, it's starting to get a little old.

The same spot in the bed. The same motions and touches leading to intercourse. The same tried-and-true position. Please! Enough! You might as well video your sex and just watch. It would be about as exciting.

It's okay to brush your teeth the same way every time. Or to empty the kitty litter the same way every time. But don't make love the same way every time.

So, lovers, loosen up in bed. It's not a business meeting. Laugh! Tickle. Wrestle. Pinch (very gently). Do some horseplay. Make funny noises. When was the last time you gave or got a hickey? It's been too long.

Try new techniques. Buy a book on sex and read it together. Experiment. "Tonight, the Northern Italian position." Nothing kinky. Nothing off the wall. Nothing either of you doesn't feel comfortable doing or doesn't enjoy. Just something different.

Shulamith asks Solomon to go with her to the countryside and make love outside (Song of Solomon 7:11–12). Now, that is outside-the-box thinking!

If you can farm the kids out, you can have sex in other parts of the house. That's the main reason for sleepovers, isn't it? To get rid of the kids so you can be alone and free to keep spicing up your sex life.

ENJOY THE POSTPLAY

The period *after* making love is *just as important* as foreplay and intercourse. Stay in bed, relax, talk about the experience, and do some more caressing, say some more "I love yous." It's the afterglow! And, husband, always keep in mind that the afterglow is a *hugely* important component of sex to your wife.

It's even possible to have intercourse again. This happens for me all the time because I'm an expert. If only! I'm past fifty now, so when I'm done, I'm done. At least for that day.

Solomon and Shulamith are masters at postplay lovemaking. Solomon stays with Shulamith after intercourse and talks in glowing terms of her beauty and how much he enjoyed their physical intimacy (Song of Solomon 5:1). After making love with Solomon, Shulamith describes their final kiss as they drop off to sleep in each other's arms (7:9).

Don't *ever* say, or even imply, "The ball game's on, gotta go." Or, "I have a chore to do." Many couples scramble out of bed so fast after making love, you'd think the bed was on fire. No! Don't do this! Linger and enjoy.

Husband, here are some ideas you can use in the afterglow. Pick up the guitar you've put by the bed, and sing her a song you've written just for her. Or read her a poem you penned for this occasion: "Violets are red, pansies are blue. I just love having sex with you."

Okay, I'm kidding. You don't have to go this far. But hang around afterward and cuddle with your dear wife. Hold her. Talk to her. Thank her for a wonderful time. This will always be a time to mention past special occasions—your first kiss, how or when you started to love her, places you've gone together. . . . She'll feel loved, and never used. And—this is important—your afterglow behavior will motivate her to desire making love with you the next time.

SEX AND THE KIDS

Having kids can ruin your sex life. It's a cruel paradox. You must have sex to have children. But once you have children, you have no more sex. It's over. Their loaded diapers, cries in the night, bad dreams, sleepovers in your house, tendency as teens to stay up late, sicknesses, and a million other child-centered scenarios rob you of your God-given right to enjoy sex.

The solution to the problem? Two simple words: boarding school. Okay, that's going too far. Actually, the solution is found in the Song of Solomon. There is no mention of children in the Song. Zero. Nada. Zilch. I think this speaks volumes.

Children are not to interfere with sex. Children are to be *out of sight and hearing* and *out of mind* during your lovemaking times.

Here are some recommendations that I am convinced Solomon and Shulamith would approve.

SCHEDULE SEX

If you have children, sexual spontaneity is not an option. You always have to work around your little—or big—darlings. Look at each week and pick the best times. Have a game plan. Carve out the time. You don't write SEX on the calendar. But the two of you look at the activities and appointments each week and decide exactly when you will have the time for intercourse. Plan it. Life with children is hectic and incredibly busy. Sex gets squeezed out if you don't schedule it.

DO IT WHEN THE CHILDREN ARE AWAKE

Don't be afraid to engage in sex when the kids are up and around. Many mothers won't have sex until the kids are asleep. Most nights, this puts sex off until too late in the evening.

"I think Timmy is finally asleep."

"Great—what time is it?"

"Midnight."

You don't have to keep your sex a secret. It's okay and healthy for kids to know what you're doing. You don't necessarily broadcast it by announcing, "Kids, we're going into our bedroom now to have sex, and you can't stop us." But it's fine to say, "Kids, we'll be in our bedroom for the next hour. Do not disturb us."

CHILDPROOF YOUR SEX

If you have the guts—and I hope you do—to enjoy sex while the children are awake, here is your battle plan.

The children are confined to their rooms or another part of the home during your time together. You don't want them huddling by your door. You've heard of those invisible fences for dogs, haven't you? The same principle applies. You tell your brood to stay on the other side of a line at least twenty feet from your bedroom door.

Don't worry about teenagers. If they think you're having sex, they may leave the country. At the least, they will retreat to the farthest corner of the home and cover their ears or turn up the volume of their music. In fact, if you ever want to get rid of a teenager who's bugging you, simply say, "We're going to have sex now in our bedroom." The teen will run screaming down the hallway.

Tell your kids not to interrupt you, except in a bona fide emergency. And it had better be good. If it's a fire, okay. If a masked man is in the home and they can't overpower him, okay. Make them believe there will be serious, painful consequences if they bother you for no good reason. They can take phone messages: "I'll have my parents call you back. They're having sex now." (I'm kidding.)

Install a heavy door with a good lock on your bedroom. The door seals in sounds and the lock provides absolute security. I've actually had grown men and women say to me with a straight face, "But we don't have a lock on our bedroom door." I reply, "Really? What can you do about that? Wait, I know. You could put one on."

Forget those flimsy little locks. The twisties and the push buttons can be defeated by a two-year-old. You want a deadbolt. I'm serious. When you swing that King Arthur door shut and slam that deadbolt home, your kids are shut out and you are secure in your fortress of love. It's a beautiful thing.

Another reason for a heavy door with a good lock is to make certain your kids don't come in and see you having sex. That would interrupt you, and it would traumatize them for life. They'll say, "What are you doing? Daddy, stop hurting Mommy!"

Finally, I recommend playing some romantic music during sex. Avoid the radio because the commercials ruin the mood. Ads for cars, laxatives, and the heartbreak of psoriasis will drain the passion right out of the room. With sex, timing is everything. Your beautiful background music is pleasant for you, it covers any sounds you make, and it prevents you from hearing the kids.

WHEN YOU STRUGGLE SEXUALLY, GET PROFESSIONAL HELP

I say *when*, because all couples struggle at times. And keep in mind: it's always *our* problem; it's never *your* problem or *my* problem. Frankly, it's just as common for the man to struggle in this delicate area as it is for the woman. You face it together, and you work through it together.

Go together to a Christian, licensed, professional psychologist who has expertise in the sexual area of marriage. In a high percentage of cases, sexual problems are symptoms of individual or relationship issues. A number of individual culprits are possible: sexual abuse as a child, unresolved issues with an ex-spouse, stress, depression, or poor self-esteem. Relationally, conflict and tension between a husband and wife can easily damage and kill their sexual relationship.

Maybe your marriage is solid but you've lost your passion and desire for each other. That's why I wrote *Kiss Me Like You Mean It* (Revell, 2009). Read it together and do the Song of Solomon–inspired exercises. The Song's relationship wisdom can bring your passion roaring back.

Sometimes sexual struggles stem from a physical problem. To be sure you've eliminated all physical causes, see your family doctor or a gynecologist or urologist. Women with muscle and nerve issues in the pelvic area can experience significant improvement via physical therapy.

Research shows that you can have a vibrant, healthy, regular sex life well into your seventies, eighties, and nineties. Now, if you're in your nineties, you might take all day to get excited. (Start after breakfast, break for lunch, enjoy orgasm by midafternoon.) But who cares how long it takes? You're retired! You have all the time in the world!

As you age, making love may take longer. That's okay.

You'll just have more time to love each other.

Solomon and Shulamith show us that sex ought to be fun. Sex ought to be intensely pleasurable. Sex ought to be a time of regular, intimate communication. This is God's design. If you follow the Song's principles, this is the kind of sex you can enjoy.

Outrageous Interaction

1. Do you both shower, brush your teeth, and smell nice prior to making love? Husband, do you shave?
2. Do you—during lovemaking—tell your spouse what you like and what feels good? Are you willing to begin communicating your sexual needs more clearly when you're in bed together?
3. Talk about your foreplay. Have you gotten into the same old rut, doing it the same old way? What would you like to do for a change?
4. Are you willing to try some new positions in intercourse? What would you like to try? (By the way, there is no Northern Italian position, as far as I know, except that which is practiced by those who live in Northern Italy. I made that one up.) There are plenty you can try. Many books have suggestions. Pick those that are acceptable to both spouses.
5. Do both of you usually have an orgasm during your sexual time together? If not, talk about how to solve that problem.
6. How is your postplay? How can you improve it? Listen to each other's suggestions and implement them.
7. Are your kids getting in the way of your sex life? What are you willing to do about it?
8. Bring up all your concerns about your sexual relationship, and begin a series of conversations to discover ways to improve in all these areas. Pray together, asking God to help you.

PART TWO

THE BAD

Lot and His Wife

OUTRAGEOUS LOVE OF THE WORLD'S PLEASURES

13
Love the World and Pay the Price

I hate movies with sad endings. If I'm going to devote two hours of my life to watching a movie, I want everything to turn out right at the end. I want the hero to win. I want all the main characters to stay alive. I want the world saved. I want the man and woman to work out their problems and live happily ever after.

Is that asking too much? I don't think so. The real world is full of sad endings. We don't need our escapist entertainment to end badly as well. I don't mind if a movie has all kinds of trouble, huge mistakes, stress, and calamity during the first hour and forty-five minutes. But in the last fifteen minutes, everything had better come up roses, or I will be royally ticked off.

For me, the movie with the saddest ending ever filmed is *Old Yeller*. This Western classic sucks you in with the story of a stray mutt that is adopted by a frontier family. This wonderful dog becomes a beloved member of the family, providing love, laughter, loyalty, and even protection. He saves the two sons by driving off a bear, attacking a wild boar, and fighting a wolf.

By the halfway point of the movie, I have fallen in love with Old Yeller. I don't even like dogs, but I want this lovable creature to be *my* dog. And then, suddenly, when I am wide open and totally vulnerable, the unthinkable happens. Old Yeller gets rabies and turns into a snarling, vicious monster. You've got to be kidding me!

Call the frontier vet! Get some friendly Native Americans to cook up a healing potion from some roots and herbs. Pray as a family around the campfire, and God can heal Old Yeller. But, oh no! Instead of using one of these reasonable and happy endings, the geniuses behind this "family entertainment" decide to kill off Old Yeller.

Worse yet, the elder son, Travis, volunteers to do the dirty deed—he shoots Old Yeller in the head! Terrible! Awful! Depressing! Then, in a lame attempt to make up for the hideous death of the greatest dog who ever lived, the movie ends with Travis bonding with a puppy sired by Old Yeller. That doesn't help me. Sorry. I don't want a new puppy. I want Old Yeller!

A Sad Story with an Even Sadder Ending

Though I really do hate sad endings, I'm going to share with you the story of a couple that has one of the saddest endings in the Bible. In fact, the entire story is terribly sad. I need to share this story because it contains a vitally important warning that God wants every couple to understand. If you heed this warning, you can avoid the disaster this biblical couple brought on themselves and their family.

Here is the story of Lot and his wife.

Awful Choice Number One (Genesis 13:1–11)

Lot and Abraham are both wealthy men with many livestock herds and servants and tents and possessions. Because the land where they are living cannot sustain them both, they decide to separate. Abraham graciously gives Lot first choice of what land to occupy.

Despite the fact that his uncle Abraham is his mentor and benefactor, Lot chooses the better land for himself. Lot is selfish. Lot is greedy. He gives no thought to what God wants him to do. He thinks only of what *he* wants to do.

Awful Choice Number Two (Genesis 13:12–13)

Lot and his wife (who is never named in the story) choose to settle in Sodom, a terribly wicked city. Sodom isn't just any wicked city. Along with its sister city, Gomorrah, it is one of the most wicked cities in the world. In the words of scripture, "The men of Sodom were wicked exceedingly and sinners against the LORD" (Genesis 13:13). The sins of these cities are "exceedingly grave," demanding punishment (Genesis 18:20). Lot and his wife should have avoided this nasty, vile place. Instead, they made a beeline for it.

They could have lived in the country, out in the hills, far away from Sodom. They could have raised their children in the knowledge of God, away from the godless, immoral influence of the city. The pitiful truth is that they wanted to be in Sodom. They were drawn to the sinful pleasures, the adulation of the crowd, the experiences this cesspool of a city offered. And they don't just live there. They become prominent citizens. Lot is appointed a judge in the city gates; obviously he has received the people's approval (Genesis 19:1, 9).

Awful Choice Number Three (Genesis 14:1–16)

Four powerful kings invade the region and capture Lot and his wife, their family members and servants, and plunder all their possessions. Abraham flies into action, rescues Lot and his entire entourage, and brings back everyone and everything.

What do Lot and his wife do after this ordeal? They move right back into good old, home sweet home, Sodom. Just as if nothing had happened. What should have been a massive wakeup call is not even a blip on the screen of their selfish, worldly minds. They have chosen to love worldly, sinful Sodom.

They should sit in ashes, repent of the sin of living in Sodom and enjoying the hedonistic, debauched lifestyle, and immediately pack up and move as far away from this hellhole as possible. Not these two. They ignore this God-given opportunity to turn their backs on the world and its sinful ways.

Awful Choice Number Four (Genesis 19:1–10)

Two angels disguised as men visit Lot at his home. All the men of Sodom surround the house and demand that Lot send his visitors out so that the men of the city can have homosexual relations with them. Incredibly, Lot offers his virgin daughters instead, so that these evil men can have sex with them, but the angels prevent Lot from sacrificing the girls.

Because of their attachment to Sodom and its sinful environment, Lot and his wife become as wicked as these sexually deviant, violent men. They zoom right by another huge wake-up call.

Awful Choice Number Five (Genesis 19:11–16)

The angels urge Lot to take his family and flee, because God has sent the angels to destroy Sodom. This is the third wakeup call given to Lot and his wife. Surely, this time they will respond in obedience and run away from this horrible city. They cannot doubt the immensity of the sin of Sodom. The angels clearly announce that they are God's messengers and that they have been sent to destroy Sodom. Lot and his wife see the angels blind the men of the city to prevent despicable sin.

But what does Lot do? He hesitates! Really? Yes, really. The angels have to literally drag Lot and his wife out of the city. Faced with certain death if they stay, they still love Sodom and don't want to leave.

Awful Choice Number Six (Genesis 19:17–26)

One of the angels tells Lot and his wife and daughters to run for their lives and not look back at Sodom. Again, they know this is an angel and that what he says comes directly from God. It's clear that to turn back means death.

So, who is stupid enough to look back? Lot's wife, that's who. She just has to turn and gaze at her beloved Sodom one last time—before God turns her into a pillar of salt. She prefers death to leaving the sinful city she loves. (It is interesting that, in speaking of the end times, Jesus warns His hearers to "remember Lot's wife" [Luke 17:32] as a cautionary example.)

The Saddest Ending Possible

Lot and his wife make six awful choices, and the results are disastrous. Though Lot is the front man, I believe his wife is involved up to her neck in every choice. The Bible does not record one word of protest from her in any of these events. Plus, because she looked back at Sodom, we know she loved the wicked city more than Lot did.

I told you this is a sad story. But it's not over yet. The last awful choice is the saddest of them all. Lot's two daughters, rather than praising God for saving them and choosing to turn back to Him in obedience, hatch an evil, incestuous plan to provide for their own security. After getting their father drunk, they have sex with him and become pregnant.

Lot and his wife's sins of selfishness and embracing the world's sinful ways are passed on to their children. The cycle of sin and disaster continues into the next generation.

Finally, Some Good News

Are you as depressed as I am at this point? I think we're ready for some good news. This terrible story serves as God's warning to every couple. As couples, we can learn four important principles from the sad story of Lot and his wife. By learning and applying these principles, we will avoid the devastation that Lot and his wife brought on themselves and their family.

Principle Number One: Don't Let the World Suck You In

Lot and his wife chose to make the world the most important thing in their lives. They chose to love the world. (This does not refer to God's physical world of beauty, but to the world system directed by Satan.) Love for the world represents mankind's sinful alienation from our Creator and is anti-God. As 1 John 2:15 says, "Do not love the world nor the things in the world. If anyone loves the world, the love of the Father is not in him." The pleasures, the entertainment options, and the enticements of the world meant everything to Lot and his wife.

If you want the best the world has to offer, you won't get the best that God has to offer.

PRINCIPLE NUMBER TWO: IF YOU LOVE THE WORLD, YOUR SINNING WILL GET WORSE

The story of Lot and his wife shows how attachment to the world and its experiences leads to greater and greater depths of sin. They chose the best land. They chose to live in Sodom. They moved back to Sodom after being kidnapped and rescued. They offered their daughters as sex slaves. They resisted leaving Sodom even when they knew God was going to destroy the city. Lot's wife chose to die rather than turn away from one of the wickedest cities on earth.

When you choose to live for the world rather than for God, your sin will take you places you never intended to go.

PRINCIPLE NUMBER THREE: YOUR LOVE OF THE WORLD WILL DESTROY EVERYONE AND EVERYTHING IN YOUR LIVES

By clinging to the world, Lot and his wife gave up everyone and everything dear to them. They lost their home and all their possessions. They lost their marriage. She lost her life. They lost their daughters to a sinful life. Most of all, they lost fellowship with God. As Sodom went up in flames, so did their lives.

The world promises you everything but ends up taking everything from you.

PRINCIPLE NUMBER FOUR: YOU CAN'T LOVE BOTH GOD AND THE WORLD

Lot tried to love God and be a righteous man (Genesis 19:2–3; 2 Peter 2:7–8). The language of 2 Peter 2:7–8 reminds us that Lot was, even at this time of his life, a righteous man.

Unfortunately, he also loved the world and enjoyed the spiritually and morally sinful pleasures of Sodom's society. On the surface, Lot seemed to be a godly man, but actually he was a hypocrite. God did not allow him to live this double life of professing faith while living in Sodom.

This period of Lot's life ends with the annihilation of his chosen home, his wealth, his companions, and all that he had, except for his two daughters. And his daughters turned out to be a pair of disgusting, sexually perverted young women. What we see is a man who means well. He is courteous (Genesis 19:1). He is hospitable (19:2–3). He knows what is good and what is evil (19:7). He is loyal (19:14). He expresses gratitude (19:19). But despite these excellent traits, he is entangled with the moral decay of this ancient sin city.

When you try to love God and the world, the world will win.

WHAT DO YOU LOVE IN THE WORLD?

I'm going to get personal now. Very personal. Hold on, because this chapter is about to become pretty uncomfortable. It's time to apply these four principles from Lot and his wife to you and your spouse.

The world has a wide variety of pleasures and attractions. Which do you love? There is one particular worldly activity that you are drawn to, isn't there?

It might be something to which you are actually addicted. Alcohol, drugs (illegal or prescription), gambling, or sex. These classic addictions are sinful and destructive in an out-front, obvious way.

But there are many other worldly pursuits that, while not inherently sinful, can certainly become sinful and destructive if you love them too much:

- children
- career
- money
- fame
- hobbies
- playing a sport

- watching sports
- charity work
- friends
- fitness
- possessions
- entertainment
- food

Ring any bells? Every activity on this list can be a healthy way to enrich your life, as long as you don't allow it to become too important and time consuming. When you love your activity more than you love God, it becomes your Sodom. It will begin its progressive march of destruction in your life.

To make it easier, I'll go first. Full disclosure. I am a workaholic. A serious workaholic. I love to do therapy. I love to do marriage seminars. I love to write books. My career is my potential Sodom.

My workaholism has hurt my marriage with Sandy, my relationship with my kids, and my relationship with God. It would have destroyed everything if I hadn't worked hard to control it. With God using Sandy and my best friend, Rocky, I keep my work in its place.

A SIMPLE SIX-QUESTION TEST
With six questions, I can determine if you are in love with the world and not in love with God.

1. How do you spend your time outside of work?
2. What do you spend your money on?
3. What are your entertainment choices?
4. How much time do you spend each week reading the Bible, devotional or teaching materials, and praying?
5. How much do you tithe to your local church?
6. How do you serve God in your local church and in parachurch ministries?

Answer these questions honestly. Then have your spouse answer them *for you*. If you are in love with the world, have the guts to admit it to yourself and to your spouse. Chances are very good that both of you are in love with a worldly activity. Just as God did with Lot and his wife, He will give you an opportunity to leave your worldly love and fall back in love with Him.

How to Get Away from the World

What you need is an aggressive plan to distance yourself from the world and grow closer to God. These steps aren't easy, but they work.

First, tell your spouse what area of the world you love too much, and describe in detail the damage this love has caused. Ask your spouse to also describe the damage your love for the world has caused. Decide that you will go through a healing and changing process *together*.

Second, each of you find an accountability partner of the same sex. This will be a person you can trust, who has your back, and who will provide encouragement and support and prayer as you change. I also recommend that together you find a couple to provide support and accountability. This couple could be the same man and woman who are your individual accountability partners.

Third, sit down together with your pastor and tell him the truth about your love for the world. Ask him to create a spiritual growth plan for you as a couple and as individuals.

At least once a week, report your progress to your spouse, your accountability partners, and your accountability couple. Describe the time you've spent on your worldly love and the time you have spent on your relationship with God. Discuss the obstacles you're facing in your efforts to change.

If your love for your worldly activity is not at an addictive level, these steps will be enough to help you recover. But if you have an addiction, you will require two additional steps: therapy with a licensed Christian counselor and a recovery group.

To find an experienced, licensed, Christian therapist, ask your pastor or call Focus on the Family (1-800-A-FAMILY) to get the name of a therapist.

Visit the counselor along with your spouse. The counselor will do a thorough assessment and develop a treatment plan. This plan will include individual recovery for the addict, couple recovery from the damage done to the spouse and to the marriage, and the rebuilding of the marriage.

Locate an addiction recovery group in your local area. You need a Christ-centered addiction group, because it will be through God's power that you will get into recovery and stay in recovery. Celebrate Recovery groups are excellent and found in many churches. Often the recovery program will include a small group for the addict and a small group for the spouse. (For more specific, detailed steps to take to deal with an addiction, see chapters 15 and 16.)

Do not take the selfish, sinful, worldly path of Lot and his wife. God gave them several opportunities to drop their love of the world and put their faith and love in Him. They blew every . . .single. . .opportunity. And it cost them everything.

This is your opportunity to leave behind your love for the world and give your love to God. He wants you to love your spouse, your children, and your friends. He wants you to enjoy healthy activities in the world. But He wants you to love Him the most and with the best of your love (Deuteronomy 6:5; Matthew 22:37; Mark 12:30; Luke 10:27).

When you love the world, you will always have a sad ending. When you love God, you will always have a happy ending.

Remember—never forget—Lot and his wife.

Outrageous Interaction

1. Tell your spouse what part of the world you love (even if he or she already knows).
2. Talk about what your worldly love is costing you: your relationship with God, your marriage, your kids, your ability to serve God, your career, time, money, etc.
3. Examine your life to see if there are any other parts of the world that you love, other than your main worldly love. Ask your spouse for his or her insight on this.
4. Discuss what you plan to do to end your love for the world and enrich your love of God. Which of my how-to steps do you need to take?

Isaac and Rebekah

OUTRAGEOUS MISTAKES IN PARENTING

14
Good People Can Be Lousy Parents

Some years ago, when it was Sandy and me and our three girls (William wasn't around yet), we drove to Orlando to spend the day at Walt Disney World. We hadn't been there for a while, and Sandy and I thought the girls would really enjoy it. As I paid several hundred dollars for our entrance tickets, it began to dawn on me why we hadn't been there for a while. That day was the longest day of my life. It still gives me the willies to think about it.

It was hot. Brutally hot. The heat came not only from the sun, but also from the body heat of the unbelievable mass of humanity clogging every square foot of the Magic Kingdom. We waited in interminable lines for everything. We waited to see Mickey and Minnie. We waited to get a drink of water. We waited for the little train that chugs around the park. We waited to order lunch. We waited until a table opened up for lunch. (I had to yell "Fire!" to clear some space.) We waited to throw out our trash from lunch. We waited to go to the bathrooms. But, most of all, we waited in line for the rides. Hours and hours of waiting for rides that each only lasted a couple of minutes.

My breaking point came at the Dumbo ride late in the afternoon. Leeann just had to go on Dumbo, so we joined the back of the line. You couldn't even see the ride from where we were. I really thought I was going to die in that line. Several folks ahead of us did collapse from heatstroke, and I silently cheered when their absence moved the line a few yards forward. (Hey, it was survival of the fittest.) After an hour and a half, we finally reached the front of the line and climbed into the Flying Dumbo vehicle. We rose and flew in a circle for a lousy, crummy, and insulting ninety seconds.

As Dumbo returned to earth, I told Leeann to stay put. When the uniformed attendant came up to ask us to get out, I said through clenched teeth: "I waited an hour and a half for this pitiful ninety seconds. We're going around again." I think that scene cost us the chance to be the featured family in the next Main Street Parade. I didn't actually have the nerve to stay on the ride. I realized I would have been torn to bits by the poor suckers still waiting for their ninety-second ride.

Leeann and I left the scene of the Dumbo nightmare and met up with Sandy and the other girls at a predetermined spot. One look at Sandy and I knew her day had been worse than mine. Nancy had thrown up all over the front of Sandy's dress. Not spit up. Thrown up. Upchucked. You could smell her thirty yards away. That was the second thing that disqualified us from being the parade family. Sandy told me later that a lady had asked her, "Did you know your child threw up all over you?" Sandy replied, "No! Really? Is that what this awful-smelling stuff is all over my dress?" There were two good results from Nancy's little accident. One, it certainly cleared a path through the crowd. Two, it brought our day to an end. Sandy said to me, "We're going home." I didn't argue.

As the five of us dragged ourselves down Main Street, Sandy and I were exhausted and in extremely foul moods. If Goofy had gotten in my way, I would have flattened him. It should have been obvious to everyone that we needed to go home. But what did my two older daughters do? Did they thank us for the day? Did they sympathize with our ragged, limp-as-a-noodle condition? Did they at least have the common courtesy to be quiet? No. Guess what they did? They cried and whined and begged to go on just a few more rides. They told us we couldn't leave Walt Disney World *early*! They said we had to stay *for them*. They wanted more fun, and we owed it to them.

This story doesn't surprise you, does it? I'm sure you could tell many similar stories. Children are selfish. Children are demanding. Children are exhausting. They believe that life is all about them and not a bit about you.

You Must Avoid Big Mistakes

Parenting is hard, brutal work. Children will drive you crazy. They're supposed to. That's their job. Your job is to maintain an intimate marriage, set reasonable boundaries, teach life skills, and raise independent individuals who love and serve God.

That's not easy. It's incredibly difficult. In our rapidly disintegrating and morally bankrupt society, the job of parenting is tougher than ever.

You will make mistakes with your children. Every parent does. You can afford small mistakes. God is gracious and kids are resilient. You cannot afford big mistakes. Big mistakes cause serious damage that lasts for years.

The story of Isaac and Rebekah and their parenting is in the Bible because God wants us to learn from their example. They made big parenting mistakes, and their mistakes devastated their marriage and their twin boys. Through this poster couple for lousy parenting, God is telling us, "Do not make these big mistakes with your kids."

Being a Good Person Does Not Mean You're a Good Parent

Before I get into Isaac and Rebekah's parenting mistakes, I want to make one thing clear: Isaac and Rebekah were good people. They were solid. They were decent. They had a strong faith in God. They were righteous.

Isaac had seen—up close and personal—the amazing faith in God that his father, Abraham, had. Isaac himself was no slouch in the faith department either. He had allowed Abraham to tie him up and put him on an altar of sacrifice. He did not resist his father and was prepared to die if that was what God wanted. He placed God's will above his own will. That's an amazing faith!

Isaac had seen God miraculously intervene to save his life and at the same time provide the ram to be sacrificed. He knew he was the miracle baby born to Sarah, his barren mother. He knew that God's blessing and promise to build a nation would continue through him.

Isaac accepted Rebekah as his wife, though he had never laid eyes on her. Though it probably helped that she was physically beautiful, he believed that God had given her to him. Again, God's will was more important to him than his own will.

Rebekah was a kind, hospitable, and gracious woman. Abraham had sent his chief servant to find a wife for Isaac. When Rebekah met this servant, she gave him water for all of his camels. She didn't have to do that. She went way out of her way to be nice.

But Rebekah was far more than just a nice person with a servant's heart. She had a strong faith in God and unquestioningly obeyed His will. She agreed to become Isaac's wife without meeting him. Why? Because she believed that's what God wanted her to do. This wasn't just a blind date; it was a blind marriage. That takes some faith!

God blessed Isaac and Rebekah with good health, great wealth, children, and protection from surrounding hostile kings and potential enemies. Initially, Rebekah was barren, so Isaac prayed, and God gave them twins. They had a blessed life, and they knew who was blessing them.

Isaac and Rebekah were faithful people who had a lifestyle of following God's will for their lives and family. Unfortunately, being faithful and obedient and righteous does not extend to their parenting decisions. As we'll see, this godly couple shows us that no matter how strong your faith in God is, if you make poor parenting choices, disaster can strike your family.

Good people can be lousy parents.

Here are the three big parenting mistakes that Isaac and Rebekah made, along with the biblical solution, a method of prevention, for each mistake.

BIG MISTAKE NUMBER ONE: PLAYING FAVORITES

As the twins, Jacob and Esau, are growing up, Isaac and Rebekah make a classic parenting mistake: they play favorites.

> *When the boys grew up, Esau became a skillful hunter, a man of the field, but Jacob was a peaceful man, living in tents. Now Isaac loved Esau, because he had a taste for game, but Rebekah loved Jacob.*
>
> GENESIS 25:27–28

Isaac prefers Esau because they both love to be outdoors and hunt. Rebekah prefers Jacob because, like her, he is a homebody—or, to be more accurate, a tent body.

This preference for a particular child seems reasonable, doesn't it? Is it so bad to favor a child who shares your interests and personality traits? In reality, having a favorite child is *not* reasonable, and it *is* bad. It's bad for the parents, and it's bad for the kids.

How bad is it? The story of Isaac and Rebekah and their twin sons reveals just how bad it is.

First, *it destroys parental teamwork*. When you have a favorite child, that relationship becomes more important than your relationship with your spouse. You make all the decisions regarding that child and give your spouse no input into how that child is raised.

By playing favorites, Isaac and Rebekah split their family into two separate alliances. Isaac is Esau's advocate, and Rebekah is Jacob's advocate. When it is time for the elderly Isaac to give his blessing, the parents work against each other and on behalf of their own favorite child. Isaac tries to give his blessing to Esau, but Rebekah hatches a scheme to ensure that Jacob receives the blessing instead of Esau.

Second, *it causes a poor relationship between the favored child and his other parent.* Rebekah is not close to Esau. Her scheme to get Isaac's blessing for Jacob does great damage to Esau. Rebekah could care less about Esau and has no concern for how her actions will wound him. Isaac has a distant, poor relationship with Jacob and is easily tricked into giving the blessing to Jacob. If he had been closer to Jacob, there's no way he would have been deceived into believing that Jacob was Esau.

Third, *it worsens the negative traits of the favorite child.* If you coddle your favorite child and don't call him on his weaknesses, those weaknesses will remain and get worse over time.

Esau's selfishness, lack of self-control, self-indulgence, self-gratification, and focus on his physical desires go unchecked by Isaac. Esau sells his precious birthright to Jacob for a single pot of stew! Later on, Esau breaks God's law by marrying two foreign women. These marriages cause great pain for Isaac and Rebekah. (Hebrews 12:16 describes Esau as immoral, but, more importantly, "godless" or profane.)

Jacob is a liar, a deceiver, and a manipulator. His name means "heel catcher, trickster, supplanter" (Genesis 27:36). He'll do anything to get ahead in life. Rebekah, far from trying to help him eliminate these awful traits, actually encourages Jacob to develop them more fully. Jacob lies to his father and scams Isaac into giving him the blessing.

Fourth, *playing favorites turns your children into enemies.* They become vicious competitors and are willing to lower themselves to any level to better themselves and be more successful. There is bitterness. There is resentment. There is hatred. And they can remain enemies for years.

Jacob wounds Esau deeply by stealing his blessing. Esau hates Jacob for this despicable action and swears to get revenge (Genesis 27:41). They remain bitter enemies for years.

BIBLICAL SOLUTION: LOVE EACH CHILD THE SAME
Every child in your family, biological, adopted, or blended, is

precious and deserves a full measure of your love. Period. No exceptions. No excuses. You need to push through every obstacle and do your very best to love and nurture each child equally.

God loves us, His children, with the same sacrificial, unconditional love. He does not play favorites. God sent His only Son, Jesus, to die for all of us (John 3:16). Not some of us. All of us. God hates favoritism and wants everyone to be treated equally (James 2:1–9).

It's easy, and natural, to feel closer to a child who has a similar personality, shares your interests, or is compliant and obedient. You must work harder to be close to a child whose personality clashes with yours, who does not share your interests, or who is rebellious. So? Work harder. And never stop working harder to build a relationship with a difficult child.

Don't do the father-son and mother-daughter thing. Dads who favor their sons and give them more time and attention do great damage to their daughters. Moms who favor their daughters do great damage to their sons.

In a blended family, it is vitally important that you never stop trying to build good relationships with your stepchildren. When you marry someone who has children, it's a package deal. Your job is to keep on loving your stepkids, and loving them, and loving them, no matter how they respond.

Stepkids can be rejecting, critical, and mean. They can be cold and withdrawn. They can ignore you. They can try to break up your marriage. They can hate you. They can want you to die or at least go away. Whatever.

Keep on loving them, and try to build a relationship. Show interest in their interests. Do the things they want to do. Give them compliments. Say "I love you" every day. Go to their sports and activities. Continually *do* loving behaviors and *say* loving things.

By loving your stepkids, you show a deep love for their parent, your spouse. Your spouse will notice your efforts and love you for trying. Loving your stepkids will eventually pay off. As adults, they will often warm up and appreciate how you never gave up on them.

One of the saddest things I ever hear in my office is when a stepparent says to me: "I'm giving up on that kid. I'm done trying to build a relationship." Don't ever say that. If you have said it, take it back now, and start trying again. It is always all right to go to God and say, "I'm at the end of my rope. Please help me to hang on. Please help me to keep trying." You are the adult. Act like it. And with God's help don't stop expressing love to your stepchildren.

BIG MISTAKE NUMBER TWO: WHEN THE PARENTS SIN IN MAJOR WAYS

Isaac is weak. He is passive. He protects himself at all costs. Just as his father, Abraham, did with Sarah, he lies and says that Rebekah is his sister (Genesis 26:7). Isaac wants to save his own hide, so he throws his beautiful wife to the wolves. Not too impressive. In fact, sinful.

It's bad enough that Isaac is a liar, a deceiver, and a manipulator, but he also abdicates the role of leader in his home. He loses Rebekah's respect by exposing her to danger. He allows her to be the leader in their relationship and in the home. When a husband and father fails to lead, he is sinning.

Isaac deliberately sins by choosing not to follow God's plan for Jacob and Esau. Despite knowing that God intended for Jacob to receive the blessing (Genesis 25:23), Isaac still attempts to give his blessing to Esau (Genesis 27:1–4). Stubborn and willful and selfish. And sinful.

But Isaac does not corner the market on parental sin. Rebekah is neck and neck with her husband in the sin category. In a shocking display of lying and conniving and manipulating behavior, Rebekah guides Jacob in a daring scheme to fool the aged and vision-impaired Isaac into giving her favorite son the family blessing. Talk about a selfish, ruthless, and controlling woman. She disrespects and humiliates Isaac, and, much worse, she usurps God's authority in order to get

Jacob the treasured blessing.

Would you like to guess how many of Isaac's and Rebekah's sinful traits and behaviors are passed on to their two sons? *All of them.* Esau is selfish, passive, irresponsible, and prone to reckless behavior. He turns from God and focuses on his own will and needs. In a stunning show of sinful pride and selfishness and disobedience to God, he marries two foreign women (Genesis 26:34–35).

Jacob becomes a selfish, deceptive, and manipulating liar. He does anything to get his way. He shows brazen disrespect for God and his father by tricking Isaac into giving him the blessing of the firstborn. He could have told Rebekah, "Mom, I refuse to fool Dad into giving me the blessing. Let's let God do it His way." But he doesn't do that. He wants the blessing and all it entails. He wants it badly, and he jumps at the chance to get it, even though it is outside of God's plan.

As we saw in chapters 5–8, Jacob is incredibly passive with his two wives, Leah and Rachel. He refuses to lead, which causes terrible pain and damage in his family. Who does this sound like? Dear old Dad and Mom!

BIBLICAL SOLUTION: LIVE A GODLY LIFE, FREE OF MAJOR SINS

As a parent, it is essential that you model a godly life for your children. What you do has much more impact than what you say. No parent is perfect, and you will sin. But your responsibility is to avoid major sins. It is your major sins that traumatize your children. It is your major sins that will show up in your children's lives.

Every parent has a weakness, an area of sin that has the potential to do great harm to their children. Mine is workaholism. What's yours? Alcohol, drugs, sexual sin, gambling, anger that is inappropriately and harmfully expressed, food, perfectionism, financial irresponsibility. Maybe it is one of the major sins of Isaac and Rebekah: passivity, lying, manipulating, failure to lead, selfishness, controlling behavior, or disrespect.

Admit your weakness and start an aggressive campaign to get emotionally and spiritually healthy. Ask your spouse, an accountability partner, your pastor, and maybe a Christian therapist to help you keep your potential sins at bay and to stay in recovery and victory. The hearts and minds and future of your children are at stake.

BIG MISTAKE NUMBER THREE: HAVING A CHILD-CENTERED MARRIAGE

As Esau and Jacob grew up, Isaac and Rebekah chose to make the children the center of their marriage and home. It's all about the two boys and who will win the blessing competition. The marriage takes a backseat to the twins. Actually, it's worse than that. Their marriage gets dumped out of the car and is left behind.

By the time the blessing scam is carried out, Isaac and Rebekah's marriage is in a pathetically weak condition. There is certainly no respect and probably very little love left. They have given up their marital intimacy and partnership in favor of meeting the needs of their sons.

How do I know their marriage is in such awful shape? Because of the terrible story of Rebekah and Jacob stealing the blessing from Esau, the older son.

First, Isaac and Rebekah do not communicate about how the blessing is to be bestowed. They both know it is God's intent to give the blessing to the younger son, Jacob. But they do not discuss this critically important issue. They do not look for God's guidance to make a plan that will honor God's will and protect both sons. Instead, when Isaac grows old, they each secretly try to get the blessing for their favorite son.

Second, Rebekah's actions reveal a deep disrespect and scorn for her husband. Her treachery and betrayal of Isaac devastate him, but she could care less. Why? Because Jacob was far more important to her than her husband. Her behavior inflicts terrible wounds on Isaac, Jacob, and Esau. These wounds remain, and fester, for years.

BIBLICAL SOLUTION: MAKE YOUR MARRIAGE THE PRIORITY

The Bible makes it clear that marriage is the most important human relationship. Marriage is "one flesh," a complete union of husband and wife (Genesis 2:24). This concept never changes and is repeated in the New Testament (Ephesians 5:31). Marriage is the very picture of Christ's relationship with the church (Ephesians 5:25, 32). Okay? Case closed. Marriage is number one.

Nowhere in the Bible does a relationship with a child reach the level of importance and sacredness of the marriage relationship.

I have heard many times from spouses in both original and blended families: "Doc, my kids come first; my kids are more important to me than my spouse. If push comes to shove, I'm choosing my kids." I always reply, "No, that's wrong. If you take that approach, you are dooming your marriage. Push *will* come to shove, and when it does, you need to choose your spouse and your marriage."

Keep your marriage strong and intimate. It is, and always will be, the foundation of the family. If you and your spouse are close and in love, you will make an excellent parenting team. You'll be able to make good, godly decisions that will benefit your children. You will be able to maintain a healthy family when the storms of life come. Plus, you will model your joy and fulfillment and teach your children how to build great marriages of their own someday.

1. Honestly, is one of your kids your favorite? Give your answer, and then ask your spouse if he or she thinks you have a favorite. If either of you answers *yes*, talk together about what poor results or damage this has caused and how you plan to make changes.

2. If you are in a blended family, talk together about your struggles to build a relationship with your spouse's kids. What are the obstacles? Discuss how you can get your relationship with your stepkids back on track.

3. What is your area of weakness? What sinful behavior tendencies have the potential to greatly damage your marriage and family? What steps are you willing to take to stay emotionally and spiritually healthy and keep this sin out of your life?

4. Do you have a child-centered marriage? Is your relationship with your children more important to you than your relationship with your spouse? Talk about how you will work as a team to nurture your marriage and make it the number one relationship in your home. . .and in your lives.

Samson and Delilah

OUTRAGEOUS LUST

15
Be Crazy in Love, Not Crazy in Lust

An epidemic of sexual sin is sweeping across America and the world. It is striking down millions of good men. Men who love Jesus Christ and serve Him in their local churches and in a variety of other ministries. Men who love their wives. Men who love their children and grandchildren.

The use of pornography among Christian men is skyrocketing. The incidence of emotional and physical adultery among Christian men is up—way up. Satan, who controls the media, is doing all he can to pump out sinful sexual material through every possible outlet: regular television, streaming services, movies, magazines, newspapers, billboards, radio, the internet, and all the electronic devices connected to the internet.

Satan is no fool. If he can entice a Christian man to fall into sexual sin, a chain reaction of damage will result. The man will be damaged. His wife will be damaged. His marriage will be damaged. His children will be damaged. His local church will be damaged. And the cause of Christ will be damaged.

I can hear Satan laughing his evil head off right now because so many Christian men are committing sexual sin. Satan is winning in this area, and he loves it.

I say enough is enough. It's time to fight back. To shut Satan up. To push back against this tidal wave of sexual immorality.

We are going to fight back by using the story of Samson and Delilah. This sad, sordid story is God's warning against sexual sin in a man's life. Samson's story reveals, in detail, the stages of sexual addiction. Understanding these stages will help you start to win the battle against your own sexual sin.

This chapter will help you determine where you are on the slippery slope of sexual sin and teach you how to get off that slope and into your individual recovery. The next chapter will show you how to heal your marriage from the traumatic impact of your sin.

Two important clarifications: Though not many women are sexual addicts, they are engaging in emotional and physical adultery in increasing numbers. And though these chapters focus on sexual sin and addiction, the principles apply to all addictions: alcohol, prescription and illegal drugs, food, work, and gambling.

STAGE ONE: GOD'S ORIGINAL PLAN (JUDGES 13:1–5)

Samson is destined by God to deliver Israel from their hated enemies, the Philistines. Before Samson is even conceived, the angel of the Lord tells his mother that her son will be God's warrior against the Philistines.

God's Message to You in Stage One

God has a special plan for your life. Before you were conceived, God knew what He wanted you to accomplish for His kingdom and His glory. If you choose to engage in sexual sin, *you* will derail this plan. It won't surprise God, but you will suffer the great loss of not fulfilling your potential as one of God's warriors.

STAGE TWO: DRIFTING FROM GOD AND OBJECTIFYING WOMEN (JUDGES 14:1–7)

Samson makes the first of many choices to disobey God and gets off track sexually when he disobeys God's law by choosing to marry a Philistine woman. (This woman is not Delilah. She comes along later, after Samson is fully ensnared in his sexual sin.) What was he thinking? The Philistines are Israel's bitter enemies! He should not be within ten miles of a Philistine woman. By his actions, Samson is saying to God, "I want to do things my way, not Your way."

He chooses his wife solely because of her physical beauty. His relationship with her is based on lust and lust alone. He inappropriately says to his father, "Get her for me, for she looks good to me" (Judges 14:3). A few verses later, scripture reinforces that Samson is interested in this woman only for her looks: "He went down and talked to the woman; and she looked good to Samson" (Judges 14:7). Something tells me there was not a lot of meaningful dialogue going on.

Samson is already objectifying women, focusing only on their bodies. This Philistine babe is physically beautiful, but she is a Philistine. She does not believe in God. And as Samson finds out very soon, she is a first-class witch.

God's Message to You in Stage Two
Husband, stay close to God. The most important relationship in your life is your relationship with God. Spend time with God every day, just you and Him. In this private time, pray and read the Bible. Attend a local church and get involved in the men's ministry. Find at least one man who will hold you accountable for your spiritual life and your sexual life.

Every man is at risk for sexual sin. If you say you are not at risk, you are either a liar or in denial. God is telling you, through Samson, that drifting from Him is the first step on the road to sexual sin. So don't drift. If you have drifted, come back to God.

The second step toward sexual sin is objectifying women. Seeing females as only a collection of body parts feeds your lust. With this one-dimensional view, women exist only to give you sensual pleasure. You see little real value in them.

Women are so much more than just physical bodies. Just like men, they have unique personalities, character traits, moral attributes, and spiritual qualities. Seeing a woman as a whole person greatly reduces the lust quotient. Samson does not care about this Philistine woman as a person, and it costs him dearly.

You need to care about every woman as a person, or you will drag yourself further and further into sexual sin.

STAGE THREE: GETTING ATTACHED TO A WORTHLESS WOMAN (JUDGES 14:15-20)

Samson's beautiful wife turns out to be a lying, manipulating traitor. What a shock! The big dummy should have known better. But, hey, she is one gorgeous babe! That's all that matters when you choose a woman, right? Wrong, as Samson finds out.

When push comes to shove, as it always does, his wife sides with her friends and throws Samson under the bus. She tells her friends the meaning of Samson's riddle, and it costs him some serious material possessions. He responds by rejecting her, leaving her, and not consummating the marriage. What a wonderful relationship.

What could go wrong by choosing a beautiful woman who does not believe in God and is part of a people group that is your worst enemy? Actually, everything could go wrong, and it will go wrong.

God's Message to You in Stage Three

Avoid all women who would entice you away from your precious wife. These women may be physically beautiful, but they are dangerous. They are the enemies of your marriage. They will destroy you. In Proverbs, Solomon writes, "The lips of an adulteress drip honey; and smoother than oil is her speech; but in the end she is bitter as wormwood, sharp as a two-edged sword. Her feet go down to death" (Proverbs 5:3–5).

Any woman who would consider joining you in sexual sin is not a quality woman. She is a home wrecker. A sleazeball. She is spiritually and morally bankrupt.

And, husband, if you consider joining a woman in sexual sin, you are not a quality man. You are just as sinful as she is.

Establish clear, unbreakable boundaries with all women

outside your marriage. Do not have personal, one-on-one conversations with a woman. Never talk about your marriage with a woman, other than to briefly say you have a great marriage and a great wife. No personal phone calls or texts or emails with a woman. Never have a one-on-one meal with any woman other than your wife. Never get into a car alone with a woman.

Obviously, if you work with women, some level of interaction is required. But keep these relationships strictly business. Do you know how many adulterous relationships begin in the workplace? Too many to count.

Women who appear in pornographic images and videos are to be avoided at all costs. Even though you will never meet them in person, it is very easy to become attracted to them in the sinful world of fantasy. See them as nasty, wicked, and poisonous creatures who want to ruin you.

Guard your eyes from sinful, sexual images. Block all television channels that have questionable, "adult" content. Put filters on your computer and other electronic devices. As perhaps never before, with the advent of the computer, anyone can engage in voyeurism, watching pornography, without *anyone knowing,* including your own spouse. It is *not* a victimless sin; and you are far from being the only victim. Such viewing is not only grievous sin and offends God, but it cripples a married couple's hope of a satisfactory, pleasurable, intimate sexual relationship. In order to pursue pornography or voyeurism, God must be put out of your mind, because these sins are inconsistent with His holy character. And do not allow your mind to indulge in sexual fantasies unless they are about your wife.

Be accountable for your sexual life to at least one godly man.

Dwell on your wife and her beauty: physically, emotionally, mentally, spiritually. "Drink water from your own cistern and fresh water from your own well. . . . Rejoice in the wife of your youth" (Proverbs 5:15, 18). Watch *her* undress. Watch *her* take a shower. When I watch Sandy without clothes on, she says, "What are you looking at?" I say back, "Who do you think I am looking at? I'm looking at you, baby, and I like what I see."

Using the other chapters in this book, work on your marriage and build real intimacy. The closer you are to your wife, the less likely you are to think about or get involved in sexual sin. Your wife is the most beautiful woman in the world. She is the most beautiful physically. She is the most beautiful person in her character and personality. She is the most beautiful spiritually (and you will have a distinct part in her spiritual growth). Think this every day, and tell her every day she's the most beautiful woman.

STAGE FOUR: LIVING THE GOOD LIFE BUT STILL SINNING (JUDGES 15:1–16:3)

Does Samson learn his lesson from his worthless, traitorous wife? No, he does not. He stays on the sexual sin train, rejecting what he knows about God and what God would have him do. In this stage of his life, he goes from a sexual sinner to a sexual addict. He goes from periodically dipping in the pool to diving in and staying in the pool.

Though Samson is hooked on his sexual activities, God, who called him from before his birth, continues to bless him. God helps him burn the grain fields of the Philistines. God helps him slaughter many Philistines in retaliation for them killing his wife. God helps him kill one thousand Philistines with the jawbone of a donkey. God saves his life by miraculously providing water for him.

What does Samson do in the midst of all these blessings from God? He spends the night with a Philistine prostitute. Really? Yeah, really. Instead of punishing him, God allows Samson to escape his enemies. Samson actually carries the doors of the city gate away as he leaves the prostitute's arms and evades his pursuers.

Samson is living the classic double life of a sexual addict. He is God's warrior against the Philistines and kills a ton of them. At the same time, he continues an entrenched pattern of sinful sexual activity. He does not stop his sexual sin. He is officially out of control in his sexual life.

I believe Samson thinks he is getting away with this sexual sin because God keeps blessing him in other areas of his life. He gets bolder and more arrogant in his sexual activities. His awful sexual choices do not seem to be harming him. What he misses is that God is not mocked (Galatians 6:7). When you disobey God's laws, you pay the consequences.

God's Message to You in Stage Four
Don't think that because God is blessing you in some areas of your life it means He's okay with your sexual sin. He's not. He will provide consequences, and those consequences will be more serious the longer you stay in your sexual addiction.

Your addiction is now a big part of your life. You do it regularly. You live for the rush of pleasure and excitement it gives you. You feel guilty afterward, but that guilt is not enough to motivate you to stop.

Your addiction is causing real damage to you and your close relationships, but you don't notice it, or care, because life is still good. You're still experiencing God's blessings; you are financially fine, your health is good. . .so your double life seems to be working. You think you can continue your secret sexual addiction and nothing bad will happen.

Disaster is looming. God is giving you a chance to repent and stop your sexual sinning. Your window of opportunity will close at a time God determines. And when it closes, it will close with a horrible, heart-wrenching, awfully destructive crash. Words can't describe how awful it will be. Just ask Samson. He can tell you. The results of his sin included horrible physical agony. Your consequences may not be physical; but, even worse, your sin may result in long-term emotional suffering for you and many others.

Now—*right now*—is the time to take aggressive action against your sexual addiction. All the steps I've recommended to this point are still important, but now you must go to another level of healing and recovery. You must mount a serious campaign against your sexual addiction if you expect to stave off the disaster that waits just around the corner.

I want you to do what I call the Big Three.

STEP ONE: CONFESSION

When we have sinned, God demands *confession* (our "saying along with Him, agreeing with Him" about our sin). Based on what Christ did on the cross and our faith in Him (Romans 10:9; 1 Peter 2:24), He will forgive us our sins and cleanse us from all unrighteousness (1 John 1:9). This is the greatest news the world has ever or will ever hear. So, Step One, confession to your wife, is an important place to start in overcoming your addiction.

Find or create a quiet, private place to talk with your wife, and then sit down with her and tell her what you've been doing to satisfy your sinful sexual desires. All of it. In detail. No, I'm not crazy asking you to do this. You're crazy if you don't do it. Yes, telling her is beyond awful and will cause her terrible pain. The only thing worse than telling her is not telling her and continuing to hide this monstrous enemy of your marital happiness.

Tell her the whole story of your use of pornography. Tell her the whole story of your emotional adultery. Tell her the whole story of your physical adultery. You are well past the initial stages of sexual sin. We're not talking about the typical temptations and occasional impure thoughts that all men face every day. These are for your accountability partners to hear, not your wife.

We're talking about a bona fide *I can't control my behavior, I keep doing it, and I can't stop* addiction. It involves regular, maybe even frequent, sinful behavior that is doing incalculable damage to you and your wife and your children.

Not telling her means continuing to lie to her. You won't change. You will continue your addictive behavior, and it will get worse. Much more damage will be done as you keep your secret. She will eventually find out, and that will trigger the disaster that God wants you to avoid. Finding out the terrible truth *from you*, though indescribably painful, is much better than her discovering the truth from some other source. By not telling her, trust and respect and forgiveness will be harder to achieve and will take longer.

Telling her the truth will create a crisis that will motivate you to change. Seeing and feeling her pain, pain you have caused, will explode the lie that your sexual addiction is not hurting her. You will never forget her reaction, and it will turn you from your sin.

As your one-flesh partner, she has a right to know. She has a right to know about this hideous cancer that is doing so much damage to her marriage and family.

Together, you can now heal. In time, once you are in recovery and with actual *tools* to keep you from committing more sexual sin, you can win her heart back and team up against the addiction.

In fact, with the entire truth on the table, genuine healing for you and her and the marriage can take place, and you can build a great marriage. You can do all this if she finds out your secret before you tell her, but it's much more difficult that way.

Step Two: Therapy
After you have confessed to your wife, find the best licensed Christian therapist in your local area and make an appointment to see him or her with your spouse. You will not defeat your sexual addiction and rebuild your marriage without the guidance of a trained therapist who is knowledgeable in sexual addiction. Let a trusted, experienced therapist guide you and your wife through the recovery process.

Step Three: Recovery
Next, find a Christ-centered sexual addiction recovery group, and attend this group for at least one year. Many churches have

the Celebrate Recovery small group program, and it is changing lives. The power of a small group is a critical piece of the recovery process.

STAGE FIVE: KILLING RELATIONSHIPS WITH EVERYONE YOU LOVE (JUDGES 16:4–31)

Samson refuses to stop his sexual sinning, so he suffers the inevitable catastrophic results. By now he has an established pattern of lusting after beautiful, foreign women of disreputable character, none of whom believe in God. The woman he married manipulated him. The second woman was a prostitute. Great taste in women. When you lust, you don't tend to be very selective.

Samson acts as if his sexual sin will never catch up with him. He is tragically wrong. He seems to believe that God will continue to bless him despite his raging addiction. He is tragically wrong.

Samson falls in love with Delilah. (He may also have married her.) But wait for it. . .wait. . .she is probably *another Philistine woman*. It's very likely that Delilah is a temple prostitute. Delilah does not love Samson. She's the type of woman who is unable to truly love a man. What she does is use men and destroy them.

Delilah takes money from the Philistine rulers to betray Samson so they can capture him. Samson, acting out of his stupidity, his lustful desires, plays games with her. He teases her and lies to her about the source of his great strength. Finally, he foolishly tells Delilah his secret. Her reaction is swift and her actions deadly.

She has his hair cut off and hands him over to his enemies. They blind him and throw him into prison.

His life is effectively over. His willful sexual sin and disobedience to God brings Samson grief and horrific affliction.

God allows Samson a final act of revenge against the Philistines. He collapses a gigantic Philistine temple in which the Philistines are sacrificing to their god, killing himself and thousands of Philistines. We can only hope that Delilah was one of the victims. This final act is far too little and far too late to redeem his wasted life.

God's Message to You in Stage Five
If you allow your sexual sin to go unchecked, it will eventually destroy you. All of your close relationships suffer as your sexual addiction continues in secret, but the huge disaster occurs when you have hidden it and it is finally exposed.

Samson loses everyone and everything because of his sexual addiction. He even loses his life. If you refuse to deal with your sexual addiction, you will suffer the same fate. That's God's message to you through Samson.

You may not die physically, but you will die in every other way: emotionally, spiritually, and relationally.

Here's what I have seen with countless husbands in my therapy office just after their sexual sin has been uncovered and things have hit the fan. Now that his appalling secret is out, he is living a nightmare. His marriage is dead. His relationships with his children are dead. His relationship with God is dead.

All these relationships can be resurrected and restored, but it is a very painful process that requires a lot of effort and time. Plan A is to address your sexual sin *now* and avoid the carnage of end-stage addiction.

Again, I urge you to tell your wife about your sexual addiction before she finds out on her own. She will be devastated and experience terrible pain, no matter how she finds out. But in my thirty years as a therapist, I've seen the benefits of telling a wife the truth up front: you get back into a close relationship with God, you stop your addictive behavior, you halt the ongoing damage to your relationships, and you get into recovery.

When you intentionally inform your wife of your own problems, she will find it easier to believe what you say about your sin—and trust will come back sooner. Not soon, but sooner. If your wife finds out on her own, she will wonder if you ever would have told her on your own—and will wonder if you are telling her the truth now.

However your wife has found out about your sexual sin—whether you told her or she discovered it on her own—you are on Plan B. The good news is that, with God's help and with hard work, Plan B can lead you into solid recovery, your wife healing from what you've done to her, and your marriage becoming restored and intimate.

The next chapter lays out the difficult but effective steps in my Plan B program.

Outrageous Interaction

1. Name several people you know who have committed adultery or been caught in some form of sexual sin. What was the impact on their lives, marriages, and children?

2. Based on your family history and personality, in what area of addiction are you prone to get involved—sex, alcohol, drugs, food, work, gambling?

3. What do you think is God's original plan for your life? What does God want you to do for Him and His kingdom?

4. Speaking only to your spouse in a private place, reveal how you are doing in the area of sexual sin. How are you dealing with sexual temptation?

5. If you are in one of the sexual sin stages described in this chapter, admit it. Are you willing to take the action steps needed to stop your addictive process and get into recovery?

16
Beat Sexual Addiction and Rebuild Your Marriage

As his wife cried silent tears beside him on the couch, the man told me his story. He was a Christian. Married over twenty years. Three kids. Regular church attender. Addicted to pornography.

Just last week, his wife had accidentally discovered the dozens of pornographic websites he had visited on their home computer. When he came home that evening and saw the look on her face, he knew something was terribly wrong. They stayed up all night talking and crying. He told me his whole life had been turned upside down. And it was his own stupid fault.

"Doc, pornography has been a part of my life since high school. It started with magazines, went to videos, spread to cable television, and now I'm hooked on internet porn. Pornography has damaged every area of my life: my marriage, my kids, my job, and my relationship with God. I've got to stop. Can you help me?"

I told this man and his wife, "Yes, I can help you. You both must be willing to work as hard as you've ever worked in your lives. God will heal each of you and your marriage through three phases of therapy."

- Phase One: The Sex Addict Gets into Recovery
- Phase Two: The Spouse Heals from the Trauma of the Sexual Sin
- Phase Three: The Marriage Is Rebuilt

Whatever your sexual sin is—pornography, emotional adultery, physical adultery—it is no longer a secret. Your spouse knows what you've been doing, and everything is a mess. Actually, much worse than a mess. Neither one of you has much hope that healing can happen.

I'm telling you that healing *can* happen. God is a God of total forgiveness and restoration. I know it's hard to believe, but my three phases of therapy can result in ongoing recovery for the sexual sinner and a better marriage for both of you than you had before. It's brutally hard work, but the benefits are worth the effort.

Let's get to work. I'll show you how I do it, using this couple as an example.

PHASE ONE: THE SEX ADDICT GETS INTO RECOVERY

First things first. The sex addict immediately gets into individual therapy with a licensed, Christian therapist who has experience working with sexual addiction. Both spouses go to the first session so the entire plan can be explained and the wife's role discussed.

I told this man I would see him in four individual sessions over the course of the next month. The purpose of these sessions is to get him onto a solid recovery path from his addiction. Everything we discussed, and all his homework assignments, would be shared by him with his wife. I had him sign a release, so I could give his wife regular updates on his progress. If he wasn't working hard, I'd tell her.

His individual therapy will continue for at least one year. When we move to couple therapy, after his initial four sessions, he remains in individual therapy. I take him through my book *I'm Not OK and Neither Are You* for the individual work.

GET A SUPPORT TEAM

In his first therapy session, I sign up his wife as a support team member. It is important that they heal together. I make two things clear about the wife's role. First, she must heal from the terrible wounds of his sexual sin before she can become a fully supportive and encouraging partner. When she is sufficiently healed and he has proved that he is well on his way to recovery, she can join him in the healing process. Until that time—I estimate it will take four to six months—he'll have to find empathy and warmth and positive words from his other support team members.

Second, she will not hear about the struggles going on in his mind. His day-to-day fantasies and temptations will be shared with his two accountability partners, his twelve-step group, and his men's Bible study group. These thoughts would overwhelm her with pain and continue to rip open the wounds in her heart. However, if he *acts out* in any sexual way, then he must tell her what he did.

For an addict, a twelve-step group isn't optional; it's absolutely critical. Addicts seldom recover without attending a weekly addiction group for a minimum of one year. The power of a Christ-centered twelve-step group cannot be overstated. I told this man to find one—and quick, which he did.

I required him to have *two* male accountability partners. Addicts are fighting patterns that are amazingly strong, so their accountability must be beefed up. He chose a close friend from church and a guy from his twelve-step sexual addiction group. He told them everything he'd done in his life in the sexual addiction area.

If at all possible, one of the accountability partners should have the same addiction as you. With a fellow addict on the job, you won't be able to fake it. You won't get away with anything, because your partner knows all the addict tricks. He'll ask the right questions. He'll notice things a nonaddict will miss. He'll understand what you're going through. He'll nail you. That's what you need.

I told my client to meet in person at least once a week with each of his accountability partners. Addiction is too strong and sneaky to be held accountable over the phone. In-person meetings are essential for at least one year.

I also told him to meet with his pastor and tell him everything about his sexual addiction and to ask his pastor to create a spiritual growth program for him that would last at least one year. Even though his faith was weak at the time, he had to start rebuilding it. This spiritual growth program might include a men's Bible study or a one-on-one discipleship relationship with the pastor or with a godly older man in the church. This man's pastor put him in a small, early morning men's Bible study. I had him tell these men his story of sexual addiction. Three more Christian men praying for him and holding him accountable couldn't hurt.

Phase Two: The Spouse Heals from the Trauma of the Sexual Sin

This man had devastated his wife. His sexual behavior left her with deep, painful wounds. One month into the process, now that he was on a good recovery track, it was time for him to help his wife heal from what he had done to her.

I made it clear to both of them that *he* was *100 percent responsible* for his sexual sin. Not 80 percent. Not 90 percent. Not 98 percent. One hundred percent. He had to own it and never, ever blame his dear wife for his sin.

Typically, this phase lasts for about three months, or ten to twelve couple therapy sessions (and positive signs appear in the marriage).

The Document of Sin

I gave the husband his first assignment—a real doozy. I asked him to write a document of sexual sin, a letter to his wife in which he described all his sinful behavior during their marriage, from their wedding day to the present, in as much detail as possible. He would read this letter out loud to his wife at our next session.

An addict must confess his sin, in writing, to the person to whom he is closer than anyone else in the world. In twenty years of clinical practice, I have seen this approach work thousands of times. In fact, I have never seen an addict recover without doing this assignment.

When the addict sees and feels the horrific impact of his sin on his precious loved one, he finally gets it. All his excuses and rationalizations evaporate. He is broken and repentant.

Now he is motivated to change. If the addict is married, this written confession will be to the spouse. If not married, it should be read to whichever family member or friend he is the closest and loves the most. It could be a serious boyfriend/girlfriend or fiancé/fiancée.

Within a marriage, this process is important for the wife's healing. The addict isn't the only one who has to recover. His wife can't forgive him until she knows exactly what happened. She can't forgive what she doesn't know. And until he tells her all of his sins, she will always wonder what actually took place. This is Trauma Work 101: Neither partner heals until the victim knows the details of the trauma.

This document of sin begins the restoration of the marriage. As the marriage is healing, the spouse can come alongside the addict, and they can become one flesh in the recovery. Plus, the intimacy they create during the recovery will meet one of the central needs of the addict, since all addictions are a search for intimacy. By going through the steps of recovery with his wife, the addict will find what he so desperately needs: intimacy with God and with his marriage partner.

Here is an abbreviated version of this sexual addict's document of sexual sin:

I am so terribly sorry for all my sexual sins. I never realized how much I was hurting you with my disgusting behavior. I know now what I've done to you, and it's killing me inside. I've told you verbally what I've done, and now I'm putting it in writing.

Honey, let me say first that these behaviors are all my fault. One hundred percent my fault. You had nothing to do with my actions. I had this sexual addiction problem even before I met you, and I brought it with me into our marriage. I should have told you the truth and gotten help years ago. I chose to lie to myself and to you, and now we're both paying a huge price for my foolishness.

During the first two years of our marriage, I didn't

use any pornography. I was so happy with you and my
problem went underground. But after our first child
was born, I went back to my old ways. The stress of
fatherhood, my new career, and missing your time and
attention may have been triggers. But there's no excuse. I
decided to go back to pornography.

Our baby was about three months old when I
started staying up late watching nasty, nudity-filled cable
television shows. You'd be surprised what you can find
on TV late at night. Movies, public access shows, and
the Playboy channel were my favorites. Some of these
channels we didn't even subscribe to, but they still came
in clear enough to see. I'd usually stay up late on Friday
or Saturday nights because I could sleep in the next day.
I'd watch two or three hours, masturbate, and then come
to bed. I'm sorry. I was stupid.

I would occasionally get a pornographic magazine
or two at a certain small grocery store. No one knew me
there. This happened about once a month. I'd hide these
magazines in my briefcase and look at them when you
were out of the house or sleeping. After masturbating, I'd
throw them in a dumpster on my way to work. Dumb. So
dumb.

For about six years, on and off, I'd buy pornographic
videos from a seedy video store. About once every two
months, I'd go in and buy two. They only cost about ten
dollars each. Here are titles of the ones I remember: [He
listed them.] I'd watch these in the middle of the night,
masturbate, and then come to bed. I would then throw
them in the dumpster on my way to work the next day.

After each episode of viewing pornography followed
by masturbating, I'd feel horribly guilty. I'd beg for God's
forgiveness and promise to stop. I could last about two
weeks before I started again. I know this sounds pathetic.
The addiction had me totally under its control. It was my
own stupid fault that I didn't admit my helplessness and

get help. The truth is, I wanted to continue.

As you now know, five years ago I started viewing pornography on the internet. This opened the floodgates to my sexual sin, which was bad and harmful even before the internet. After, it became much worse. I couldn't believe how easy it was to find pornography online. The number of sites seemed endless, the variety was incredible, and most of it was free.

Magazines, television, and porno movies fell to the wayside as I got into internet porn sites. Late at night, or when you and the kids were out of the house, I'd visit these sites. I felt safe because you weren't very computer savvy. Most weeks, I'd view internet porn about every three or four days. And more on the weekends, when I had more time.

I'd spend hours, sometimes three or four in a row, surfing porn sites. Friday night, Saturday night, and usually Sunday afternoon—these were my usual times. But then I started viewing porn on weeknights as well. I couldn't seem to control myself. Here are the sites I can recall visiting: [He listed them.] I know you printed out a list of most of the ones I visited in the last three months.

I have to tell you something you don't know yet. I went to two strip clubs this last year. [He named them.] Both times, I watched the girls dance for about thirty minutes and then left. I guess I wanted the rush of seeing naked women in person. Anyway, it didn't do much for me. They weren't attractive, and I spent the whole time scared to death that someone I know would see me.

Well, that's it. I'm ashamed beyond words of what I've done. I'm sorry, so very sorry for my sin. I know I have hurt you worse than anyone has ever hurt you. I know you will have to vent your feelings and ask me questions for a while. I will listen and answer all your questions for as long as it takes. I will do whatever it takes to fix this problem and win you back. Please, please, hang *in there with me as I work through to recovery.*

When he read this letter to his wife in our session, it was very intense and very painful. It needed to be. Both were in tears before he finished. The process blew up Satan's lie that the husband's behavior wasn't hurting anyone. The healing for both of them had begun.

I instructed him to read this letter as soon as possible to his two accountability partners, his twelve-step group, his pastor, and the three men in his Bible study. I asked his wife to read the letter to her closest female friend. She needed empathy and prayer support from a trusted confidante who knew the hurts she had suffered.

THE DOCUMENT OF RESPONSE

I told his wife it was now her turn to write a letter to her husband, containing her response to what he had done to her. A letter expressing, without limitation or qualification, her emotional pain, rage, disgust, anger, resentment, frustration, sadness, terrible disappointment, and hurt. I urged her not to hold back, because full and honest release of emotion is a critical part of the forgiveness process.

She wrote ten pages straight from her heart. Here are key portions of her response:

> *I don't know if I can find the words to describe what you've done to me with your sexual sin. You have hurt me like no one else could. You have broken my heart, and I don't know if it can be healed.*
>
> *I feel like I don't even know you. In fact, I don't want to know the person who did all these miserable, hurtful actions. Here's what I do know: You have lost me. There's a good chance you won't get me back. If you want to win me back, you'd better work like no man has ever worked to change and become the godly husband I want and need.*

You see, I thought I had a godly husband. Turns out, I didn't. I had a husband who defiled himself, me, our kids, and our marriage, over and over again.

My initial shock has turned to rage. How could you keep doing these things you knew were wrong? How could you lie and deceive me for all these years? I am beyond furious at you. You have been so selfish it makes me sick. Why didn't you get help? Why didn't you tell someone?

I think of you watching naked women and I want to scream in your face, "What are you doing? You've got a wife who loves you! You can see me naked and make love to me!" But no, you took what was mine alone and gave it to these anonymous whores.

I am shaking with anger as I write these words. And underneath the anger is a terrible hurt and sadness. You have wounded me just as if you'd taken a knife and gutted me with it. You, who were supposed to protect and honor me. Instead, you've damaged me and humiliated me.

I've cried and cried and cried. I feel like I have been torn apart and don't know how I can be put back together again. I don't trust you. I don't feel safe with you. I don't know if I love you. I've taken my heart, my broken and bleeding heart, away from you.

Do your work. Follow the steps of recovery to the letter. Let me know how the process is going. Listen to me every time I want to talk about what you've done. Hear me vent and feel my pain. Answer all my questions. Grow in the Lord. You can't change without His help.

I don't offer you any guarantees. "We'll see" is the best I can do.

It was pure agony for both of them when she read this letter in our session. But it was the truth. And the truth heals. She had to say it, and he had to hear it. You'll notice there was no empathy or understanding in her response letter. It was venting about his sin and the pain he had caused her. Nothing else. Emotional expression must come first.

She was a step closer to forgiveness and to becoming a partner in his healing process.

THE MODE

The next step for the addict and his spouse was what I call the Mode, a series of brutally honest, intense, and deeply personal conversations about his sexual behavior. The spouse can ask to have one of these talks at any time, and the addict's response—every time—will always be, "Yes, let's talk."

I told the spouse that her job was to use these talks to vent her emotions as freely and completely as possible. She was also to ask all the questions that came into her head, with the exception of asking about his fantasies and temptations. In my experience, it is best to focus on his sinful *behavior*. Exploring the nasty thoughts in his mind is too painful and overwhelming for a wife. These fantasies and temptations are to be shared with the husband's sexual addiction group and his accountability partners.

His job, in the face of these confrontations, is to be attentive, patient, kind, loving, understanding, and reassuring. He is to say he is sorry a million and one times, if necessary—and mean it every time. He is to do his best to answer all her questions, even when she repeats them over and over. As they work through the rest of the recovery steps, he is to answer her specific questions about why and how he developed the addiction.

The one-two-three punch of the two documents and the Mode accelerates the healing of the addict, the spouse, and the relationship. For a more complete explanation of this approach to serious marital sin, read my book *What to Do When Your Spouse Says, "I Don't Love You Anymore."*

Phase Three: The Marriage Is Rebuilt

The couple is now four months into the healing process. Their hard work is paying off. He is on a solid recovery track. He is continuing his individual therapy with me; he is attending his sexual addiction group and his spiritual growth small group, and he is meeting regularly with his accountability partners. He has not acted out sexually in the past four months. He has a system in place to help him manage and control his sexual urges and temptations.

The wife is on a solid recovery track from the wounds he inflicted on her. Forgiveness and trust take time, but she is moving forward in these areas. His success in his recovery program, his honesty about his sin, and his sensitivity to her pain are key factors in her progress. She is not by any means fully healed. Anything near "fully" will take at least eighteen months. But she is *on her way* toward healing.

Let's Team Up

It's time to transition from "You hurt me terribly and I need to work through these hurts with your help" to "I'm ready to work with you against your sexual addiction." With the groundwork that has already been established, the wife is ready to team up with her husband to fight his addiction.

For four months, it has been his problem, and she's been struggling to heal from what he did to her. Now it needs to become *their* problem, and she will stand shoulder to shoulder with him in his ongoing recovery process.

At this point, I will give the wife a crash course in sexual addiction: where it comes from, the different forms it takes, its progressive nature, what triggers the sexual acting out, what is required to defeat it every day, and the important truth that it is a desperate search for intimacy. This education completes the base of knowledge she has already gained by being privy to the steps he's taken in his individual therapy.

The husband will battle his addiction the rest of his life. That's the bad news. There is no final cure. He'll always have to work for the cure every day. The good news is he can remain in recovery for the rest of his life and avoid sexual sin. To be successful, he needs his wife's help and support.

THE TRUTH AND NOTHING BUT THE TRUTH

In their renewed marriage, the husband will be totally honest with his wife about his *serious* struggles and temptations in the sexual area. Low-level temptations and impure thoughts will be shared only with his therapist, his accountability partners, his sexual addiction group, and his spiritual growth small group. Even when a man is walking with God and in solid recovery, he will have impure thoughts. (All men have occasional temptations and impure thoughts.) If he deals with these right away—dismissing them from his mind—there is no need to tell his wife about them.

When he hits a patch of intense temptation—if he has allowed impure thoughts to take control and is on the verge of acting out sexually—he will tell all the men mentioned above, and he will also tell his wife. She will be upset, and they will have to work through her feelings. But she will appreciate his honesty, and together they will deal with the challenge. They'll talk about it, they'll pray about it, and they will take assertive steps to defeat the temptations.

In their renewed marriage, they will both be totally honest about all areas of life and their relationship. They will express emotions, they will air grievances, and they will share specific needs. They will not tolerate any more secrets about anything.

THE I-DON'T-WANT-A-DIVORCE STEPS

I take the couple together through the seven steps in my book *I Don't Want a Divorce*: regular Couple Talk Times, the letter of responsibility, positivity, conflict resolution skills, past-pain transfer, forgiveness of each other, and meeting real needs.

In this stage, the wife is finally able to identify and work on her own weaknesses and contributions to the marital problems. Over this ninety-day, ten-to-twelve session program, they complete their healing as a couple and build a brand-new marriage. A marriage that will go the distance.

God has done what only God can do. He has used the healing steps and all the hard work to bring this couple out of utter disaster to a beautiful new reality. The husband is in a strong and (we hope) permanent recovery process. The husband is closer to God. The wife is in a strong recovery process from the trauma. The wife is closer to God. Together they are closer to God. And they have built, and will continue to build, a healthy, closer-than-ever relationship.

Outrageous Interaction

1. Build your support team: your Christian therapist; your two, same-sex accountability partners; a twelve-step group; your pastor; and a spiritual growth discipleship group or small group Bible study. Commit to getting into recovery.
2. Write your document of sin to your wife, and read it aloud to her.
3. Ask your wife to write and then read to you her document of response.
4. Begin the Mode with your spouse and agree to continue it as long as it takes to produce healing.
5. Team up with your wife against the sexual addiction. Talk about what would stop you from teaming up.
6. With a Christian therapist, work together through my ninety-day *I Don't Want a Divorce* program.

Nabal and Abigail

OUTRAGEOUS ABUSE

17
The Abusive Husband and the Victimized Wife

Abuse is an ugly word. It is an even uglier reality in many marriages. If you live with an abusive husband, these two chapters are written for you.[1] If you don't have an abusive husband, I'll bet you know someone who does and is in desperate need of this information.

Your husband is abusive if he willfully engages in an ongoing pattern of sinful behavior that significantly harms you, your children, your marriage, and himself. Here is a list of behaviors I consider abusive:

- physical abuse: punching, kicking, shoving, slapping, choking, throwing you down, not allowing you to leave a room or your home
- verbal abuse: vicious criticism, personal attacks, venomous sarcasm, profanity-laced lectures
- anger outbursts: screaming, yelling, destroying property, throwing things
- sexual abuse: forcing you to have sex against your will
- sexual addiction: pornography, physical or emotional adultery, staring at other women with lust
- financial irresponsibility: overspending, can't hold a job, refuses to find a job, failure to pay bills and/or taxes, creates serious debt

---

[1]The principles in chapters 17 and 18 also apply to abusive wives and victimized husbands.

- extreme selfishness: he meets only his own needs
- extreme control: he seeks to control every aspect of your life—your clothes, your friends, your schedule, your free time, what you can purchase
- alcoholism
- drug abuse
- gambling
- workaholism

Sound familiar? Are you tired of living with a man who consistently exhibits one or more of these outrageously sinful behaviors? I hope you are. I know God does not want you to keep living this way with this kind of man. How do I know this? Because of 1 Samuel 25, the triumphant story of Abigail and her husband, Nabal.

LIVING A NIGHTMARE

Abigail was living a nightmare. Why? The answer is one word: Nabal. One of the true dirtballs of the Bible, Nabal is a classic example of an abusive husband. Here's how the Bible describes him: "The man was harsh and evil in his dealings" (1 Samuel 25:3). *Evil* is a pretty strong word. In 1 Samuel 25:25, Abigail uses some choice words of her own to describe Nabal. Referring to "this worthless man," she says, "Folly is with him." When your own wife calls you a worthless fool, you have to be a dirtball.

When a clinical psychologist (that's me) reads 1 Samuel 25, more nasty personality traits emerge about Nabal. He was incredibly selfish. He was ungrateful. He was mean. He was bitingly sarcastic. He was arrogant. He had no empathy for others. If I had to diagnose him, I'd label Nabal a *narcissist*. He didn't care about anyone but himself. It was all about him.

As a person, Abigail was a completely different story. Even though compared to Nabal any woman would seem like a saint, Abigail was a very impressive person. The Bible calls Abigail "intelligent and beautiful" (1 Samuel 25:3). Other wonderful traits emerge from a reading of her story. Abigail had tremendous empathy. She was decisive and efficient. A natural leader. She was courageous, humble, and insightful. Nabal did not deserve Abigail. Obviously. She was a good, solid woman.

I'll tell you something else: she was stuck in a horrific marriage to a world-class creep. With no way out. In that day, a wife had no rights. She was her husband's property. A wife had two choices if she was unhappy with her husband: endure the pain and stay married to him or endure the pain and stay married to him. If a wife in those times didn't sit down and shut up, her husband could do very bad things to her. Check out the Middle East marriage scene today, and you'll see not much has changed.

Abigail was in a hopeless situation, right? Wrong! God did what God does when He wants a wife to get out of an abusive marriage. He intervened and presented Abigail with an opportunity to escape her painful, destructive marriage. Abigail stood up, spoke up, and changed the direction of her life.

Here is Abigail's story. Prepare to be amazed.

FROM NIGHTMARE TO NEW LIFE

Nabal was a very wealthy narcissist. "He had three thousand sheep and a thousand goats" (1 Samuel 25:2). In today's world, that's like having a Palm Beach mansion, a place in the Hamptons, and millions in the bank.

David, Israel's king-in-waiting, sent some of his men to ask Nabal for provisions to sustain him and his men. As part of his request for help, David had his emissaries mention the fact that he had protected Nabal's workers during the recent shearing season. Being filthy rich, Nabal could easily have given David what he needed.

Instead, Nabal refused to give David anything. True to his nasty nature, Nabal said no in a contemptuous, sarcastic, and insulting fashion. David was furious and immediately planned to storm Nabal's camp with four hundred armed men. David was going to slaughter Nabal, slaughter every male in his household, and take by force the food he needed.

When Abigail learned of David's plan, she flew into action. With the help of some male servants, she gathered a large amount of food and set out to intercept David. Her courage was remarkable in two significant ways. One, she gathered the supplies without telling Nabal. That broke all the rules of marriage in that day. Wives just didn't take that kind of dramatic, independent action. Nabal could have punished her severely for acting alone.

Two, she boldly traveled to confront a deadly, rage-filled warrior and his four hundred bloodthirsty soldiers. Talk about a risk! She literally put her life on the line. Thanks to her quick thinking and bravery, Abigail saved Nabal and her household from a massacre.

David was impressed with Abigail and blessed her for saving him from a rash course of action.

When Abigail assertively told Nabal what had happened and how close he had come to utter disaster, he suffered what was an apparent heart attack or stroke and died about ten days later. The truth is, God took him out: "The LORD struck Nabal and he died" (1 Samuel 25:38). I have a feeling Nabal's funeral was not well attended. And it was probably a time of rejoicing rather than mourning.

When David heard of Nabal's death, he thanked God for getting rid of this evil man. And he wasted no time asking Abigail to marry him. Abigail was thrilled to accept. It was certainly a strange courtship but a beautiful ending to the story.

GOD IS TALKING TO YOU THROUGH ABIGAIL

If you are married to an abusive husband, the account of Abigail's escape from Nabal is God's way of sending you a message. It is a message of hope, motivation, and practical instruction.

- Abigail was married to a mean, worthless, abusive husband.
- When Abigail's family was threatened by her husband, she took action.

- Abigail acted, not to protect her husband, but to protect her family.
- Abigail told others the truth about her husband.
- Abigail enlisted the help of others in her escape plan.
- Abigail did not tell her husband what she was doing.
- At the right time, Abigail confronted her husband with the truth.
- Her husband didn't change; Abigail changed.
- When God offered Abigail a way out of the abuse, she took it.
- God approved Abigail's assertive behavior and blessed her for it.
- Abigail got away from her husband and enjoyed a new life of freedom and adventure.

Go back and read the above section again. But this time, insert your name in place of Abigail's name. Walk in Abigail's shoes. You're already walking in her shoes, aren't you? I know you can relate to her. You are suffering every day in a marriage very much like Abigail's marriage.

Follow Abigail's gutsy example and stop tolerating your husband's abusive treatment.

God provided Abigail with an opportunity to get out of an abusive marriage. And she seized it. God, through Abigail's story, is providing you with an opportunity to get out of your abusive relationship. This is your opportunity. Right here. Right now.

You're feeling very anxious, aren't you? You're thinking, *I'm not ready. I'm not strong enough. I don't know what to do.* I know you're not strong enough now to take action. I get that. Though the Bible does not mention it, I believe God spent time preparing Abigail for action against Nabal.

Read my four-step Escape from Abuse plan below. These proven steps will get you ready and describe exactly what to do to stop the abuse. Keep an open mind, and ask God to show you if this is the approach He wants you to follow.

STEP ONE: GET OUT OF DENIAL

Every abused wife lives in denial. Denial helps you cope. It helps you function. It helps you survive each day with your lousy, sinning husband. Denial keeps you right where you are.

You make excuses. You generate rationalizations. You believe lies. You refuse to acknowledge reality. You embrace deception. The grim horror of your marriage is right in front of you, but you don't want to see it. If you did see it, you'd have to do something about it. And you are scared to death to do anything about it.

The first step away from abuse is getting out of the darkness of denial and into the light of truth. You will see the truth only when you are forced to face it. . .repeatedly. Get ready for the truth, the whole truth, and nothing but the truth. And, yes, I will add: So help you God.

Dialogue with an Abused Wife

Here is a dialogue I have had with scores and scores of abused wives over twenty-six years as a clinical psychologist. Though the type of abuse varies, the dialogue stays pretty much the same.

Wife: I'm being told by some solid Christians that the abuse is my fault because of failures on my part. They say if I were a better wife, he would change and stop abusing me.

Dave: Ah, yes, the classic Christian approach to an abused wife. These Christians may be well-meaning, but they are clueless. And wrong. And they are seriously unfair in their judgment of you. Your husband's behavior is sinful and 100 percent his fault. Nowhere in the Bible is sin blamed on anyone but the sinner. Your only fault is tolerating his sinful, abusive treatment

	of you.
Wife:	But if I were a better wife and loved him more, wouldn't he change?
Dave:	You've already been trying that approach for years! How is it going? Has he changed yet? You'll never be a good enough wife to change him, because you're the only one trying. He doesn't have to try, because he also believes it's your responsibility to make the marriage work—and, to him, you're failing. The *only way* an abusive husband will change is when his wife decides to stop tolerating his abuse and assertively requires him to agree immediately to take steps to change.
Wife:	These same Christians say that I have to submit to him, no matter how he treats me.
Dave:	You're hanging around the wrong Christians. Their view of submission is distorted. When you are married to an abusive husband, submission is suspended. The Bible teaches us not to submit to a sinner, but to confront a sinner (Matthew 18:15–17). If you submit to his sinful behavior, you are actually helping him stay the way he is. It's called *enabling*. He thinks everything's fine. He thinks he's fine. By submitting, rather than confronting him, you are sinning.
Wife:	Maybe God is punishing me for my sins.
Dave:	No, God doesn't work that way. This is another way of blaming yourself for your husband's behavior. If you have asked for forgiveness, God has completely forgiven you for your sins (1 John 1:9). You are

	playing God by punishing yourself.
Wife:	I'm so used to living this way, it's no big deal. It's not so bad.
Dave:	Now, that is sad. Very sad. Not so bad? Listen to yourself talk! It's a good thing you're in a psychologist's office, because you need help. It *is* that bad! When you're healthier, you'll realize that being abused is not normal.
Wife:	My husband really loves me.
Dave:	No, he really doesn't. He's not even close to the biblical definition of love found in 1 Corinthians 13. He's supposed to love you "just as Christ also loved the church and gave Himself up for her" (Ephesians 5:25). How is he doing, measured by this standard? I can make a strong case that your husband hates your guts. Your worst enemy wouldn't treat you this badly. He doesn't know how to truly love anyone. We'll see if he's willing to learn how to love.
Wife:	He had a bad childhood, so he can't help how he is acting.
Dave:	That's no excuse for sinful behavior. Plenty of husbands have had bad childhoods and don't abuse their wives. If he chooses to work through his childhood pain, he can heal and be a different husband. He may do this work if he loses you.
Wife:	He can't handle stress, so he acts out against me.
Dave:	Tell him, "Welcome to the real world, where big boys have to learn how to handle stress." We all experience stress.

His problem is not stress. His problem is that stress triggers his deeper issues, and these have to be dealt with.

Wife: My husband says he's not abusing me. He says I'm overreacting.

Dave: He's a liar, and he believes his lies. He's in denial. Of course he doesn't think he's abusing you. If he admitted to abuse, he'd be wrong, and he's never wrong. By denying abuse, he's being abusive. *You* define what is abuse, not him. As you get stronger, he's going to accuse you of some *serious* overreactions.

Wife: He says he's sorry after he abuses me.

Dave: He's not sorry. People who are genuinely sorry stop the mistreatment. His "apologies" aren't doing you any good, are they? If I keep running you over with my car, is it okay as long as I say I'm sorry each time? You don't need to hear one more lame apology. You need him to change.

Wife: He promises he'll never mistreat me again, and I believe him.

Dave: I'll bet you also believe in the Tooth Fairy. How many times has he promised to stop abusing you? Without hard work on his personal issues, which it's unlikely he'll do, he'll never change. His promises mean nothing. Believe him only when you observe real, lasting change.

Wife: Doesn't the Bible teach me to forgive him?

Dave: Yes, it does. We are always to forgive those who sin against us (Matthew 18:21–22; Luke 11:4). So, you need to forgive him for all his abuse. But forgiveness does not include tolerance of ongoing sin. You forgive the sinner, but you also follow the Bible's teaching to confront the sinner and require changed behavior (Matthew 18:15–17; 1 Corinthians 5:1–13).

Wife: Aren't I supposed to stay with him "for better or worse"? Maybe this pain is God's plan for me.

Dave: "For worse" does not mean living with an abusive husband. I guarantee you this is not God's plan for your life (though He can use such trials to mold us). God's plan for you is the same plan he had for Abigail: stand up to the abuser and demand change.

Wife: I'm staying with him because it's better for the kids.

Dave: The brutal truth is, you are ruining your kids. You are allowing their precious self-esteem and confidence to be shredded. You are teaching them that it's okay, it's normal, for a husband to abuse his wife. They may have sadness, but no respect for you, and they will follow their father's example and mistreat you. It is likely that your boys will abuse their wives. Your girls will likely marry abusive men. And that will be on your conscience.

Wife: I still believe he can change.

Dave: Maybe he will change, and maybe he won't. In my plan, he'll have his chance to change. The best and only chance you have for his changing is by your changing the rules and demanding that he change. An abusive man changes only when it's the only avenue to getting his wife back. It's not about him anymore, though. It's about you and your children, whom he promised to love and protect. It's time to protect yourself and your kids from further damage.

Wife: I believe God wants me to stay with my husband even if he doesn't change.

Dave: You're the one who wants to stay. God didn't want Abigail to stay, and He doesn't want you to stay. If you are foolish enough to remain with your abusive husband, there are only three possible outcomes: You will stay miserable for your entire marriage and you and your children will be severely damaged; your husband will grow tired of living with a doormat and dump you for another woman; or you will eventually lose all love for him and divorce him. These outcomes prevent you and your children from finding domestic happiness and prevent the possibility of your husband's reforming and becoming a devoted follower of Christ and loving husband and father.

Wife: You think I'll want to leave him one day and get a divorce?

Dave: It's entirely possible. When you lose your love for him and hit the wall, you won't care if he changes. You'll be done. And this will be after you have missed perhaps *years* of happiness. Act now while you still love him and can respond if he changes.

Wife: If the truth about our unhappy marriage comes out, it will be humiliating.

Dave: So, you're saying your pride is more important than saving yourself and your kids? Your pride is more important than giving your husband an opportunity to change? When your life is ruined and your kids are messed up as adults, you can comfort yourself with the knowledge that at least no one knew about the abuse. If you divorce, *everyone* will hear of it.

Wife: I can't make it on my own. Standing up to him is too hard and too risky.

Dave: Philippians 4:13 states: "I can do all things through Him who strengthens me." You either believe the Bible, or you don't. You either believe that God is able to give you the strength you need, or you don't. You're not strong enough today, and you won't be strong enough tomorrow. But, with God's help, you can get strong enough to do what has to be done to be free of the abuse. Remember, Abigail was in a much more dependent and helpless position than you are, and she broke through to a new life. God helped Abigail, and He's going to help you.

Wife: I can't do this alone!

Dave: I know you can't. You don't have to. You're going to have help and plenty of it. In fact, creating your support team is the next step in my Escape from Abuse plan.

Outrageous Interaction

1. It's time to be honest with yourself. Are you living with an abusive spouse? By saying yes, you've begun the journey to freedom.
2. Specifically, what type of abuse have you experienced? How long has the abuse been going on?
3. What is the impact of the abuse on you? What is the impact on your children?
4. How is your husband like Nabal? How are you like Abigail? What feelings and thoughts in you does Abigail's story bring out?
5. With which parts of the "Dialogue with an Abused Wife" can you identify? What are the top three things that keep you in your enabling role with your abuser? What do you fear the most about taking a stand against your abuser?
6. Before you read the next chapter, which contains the final three steps in my Escape from Abuse plan, pray that God will be with you and speak clearly to you.
7. If you are not an abused wife but know someone who is, commit to take three actions: tell her you know she's an abused wife, ask her to read chapters 17 and 18 in this book, and assure her that when she's ready to do my plan, you will be on her support team.

18
Enough Is Enough

If you're still reading, I haven't lost you yet. Good. These steps I am explaining are tough to read. And tough to do. But they are the way out of abuse.

Maybe you will make the decision to stay in your abusive marriage. You have that choice. You have free will. But my hope and prayer is that you will choose to follow these four steps and get out of the abusive cage of your marriage.

Whatever you ultimately decide, all I ask is that you read this chapter, pray for God's guidance, and then make your decision.

STEP TWO: GET YOUR TEAM READY FOR BATTLE

No one ever escaped an abusive relationship alone. No one. Abigail didn't get out by acting on her own. She had help. You also need help to conquer your fears and your feelings of false guilt and take assertive action. Don't waste your time trying to escape the abuse alone. You'll never make it.

The phrase "one another" is found fifty-eight times in the New Testament. Fifty-eight times! God makes it clear that we need other people. The Bible is filled with verses instructing us to support, love, encourage, confront, and be accountable to one another.

Every team member must be a strong, unwavering supporter of your decision to no longer tolerate the abuse in your marriage and to fight back against your sinning husband. You don't need a team member who tries to see things from your abusive husband's point of view. You don't need a team member who wants you and your husband to get marriage counseling. This isn't a marriage counseling situation. At least not yet. It is a case of an abused wife taking a stand and saying, "Enough is enough," and forcing her husband to make a choice: "Change or lose me."

You don't need a team member who recommends the "keep on loving him, and he'll eventually stop abusing you" approach. It's not biblical. It doesn't work. It's dangerous. It's like telling someone to keep on trying to charm a deadly cobra as it repeatedly bites her. You know what you ought to do? Get away from the cobra!

Avoid all the passive, hand-wringing, wimpy, gutless enablers. They are everywhere, and their advice will only lead to a continuation of your abusive relationship. These ignorant, clueless people don't get it and probably never will.

What you need is a team of fellow warriors in your battle against the abuser. Each team member will read these two chapters (17 and 18) and endorse my escape plan. Each team member will commit to staying with you all the way to the end of the campaign.

Here is your team.

God

Your most important team member is God. Why? Because He is the only one who can give you the power, wisdom, determination, and protection required to deal with your abusive husband. God will walk with you through every step of my proposed Escape from Abuse plan. With His presence and supernatural support, you will get the job done. Actually, *God* will get the job done through you.

Be like Abigail. Abigail leaned on God throughout her escape from Nabal's abuse. When you read Abigail's plea for mercy to David (1 Samuel 25:23–31), you see a woman who believed in God. A woman who had a close relationship with God. Who knew God was intimately involved in her crisis. Who trusted in God to save her and her household. Who put her life and future in God's hands.

To stay close to God and experience his full support, you need to spend personal time with Him every day. Meet with God for fifteen to thirty minutes in the morning, afternoon, or evening. Use a private, quiet place. Allow no distractions or interruptions.

When it's just you and God together, pray to Him. Vent your fears and feelings. Thank Him for what He's done for you and what He's going to do for you. Make specific requests. And then be quiet and listen to Him—that is, let your mind concentrate on Him; let Him focus your thoughts on what He wants you to do. Let your mind go to Scripture verses you have learned or you have read, and meditate on them. Talk with God throughout the day to maintain your intimate bond and draw on His strength.

Make sure you read the Bible in every private time with God. When you read the Bible, God is able to speak directly to you through the text. There is nothing more powerful in the universe than God's Word. The Bible will sustain you, encourage you, and guide you. Read Abigail's story over and over. Her story is your story. What God did for her, He will do for you.

Your Accountability Partner
You need a solid, trustworthy, and loving Christian woman to walk with you, right beside you, through these difficult steps of escape from abuse. She must have a strong, personal relationship with Jesus Christ and be growing in that relationship. You must be able to trust her to keep everything you tell her confidential.

She will meet with you in person at least once a week to provide spiritual and emotional support. She'll be available 24-7 by phone. She will pray with you. She'll cry with you. She'll laugh with you. She'll share your pain. She'll encourage you and motivate you. She will not let you quit or lose heart, or give in to the abuser's pleas, and she won't let you stop your implementation of the plan. She will not give up on you.

If you attend a church—which is what God wants you to do (Hebrews 10:25) as part of His way for you to grow in your faith—ask your pastor or his wife for names of potential accountability partners. You may find a woman who has already been down the road you're on and has achieved freedom from an abusive husband. Pray that God will lead you to the right woman. God knows who she is, and He'll get the two of you together.

Family and Friends
Tell your family and your close friends the truth about your husband. They may already know about or suspect the abuse. Or they may not have a clue because you've covered up the truth so well. Your days of lying to protect your husband are over. Your family and friends need to know what's been happening in your marriage, and they need to know now.

Abigail enlisted the support of the young men of her household (1 Samuel 25:14–19) and told David the truth about Nabal (1 Samuel 25:23–31). Share the truth only with family and friends whom you are confident will understand your painful situation and support you 100 percent. If your parents, siblings, or other family members have never supported you or have even mistreated you, don't bother reaching out to them. Just tell your friends.

At this point, don't talk to your husband's family or friends. They most likely will support him and blame you.

Your family and friends can provide critical spiritual and emotional support, as well as practical support: babysitting, financial help or advice, assistance in finding a job, and possibly providing a safe place for you to live temporarily. Down the road, in my plan, they may be involved in confronting your husband.

Your Pastor and Your Local Church
If you are not regularly attending a local church, you're in trouble. Right now, in the face of all the abuse you've encountered, you are not only emotionally weak and vulnerable but also spiritually weak and vulnerable. Therefore, I cannot overstate the power and life-changing influence of a strong local church and pastor.

Church is where you worship God with others, a practice established in the New Testament. Church is where you serve

God. Church is where you find peace and sanctuary in your stressful, often painful world. Church is where you can learn to grow closer in your relationship with God. Church is where you will find quality friends who will support you as you escape your abusive marriage.

Sit down with your pastor—or an associate pastor if you attend a large church—and tell him everything. He will be an invaluable spiritual guide during this time of crisis. Your pastor will comfort you, guide you, encourage you, pray for and with you, and call on the many resources of the church to assist you.

A Small Group

I urge you to join a small group. Most likely, the small group will be connected to your church. In this kind of group, you can truly connect with others. You'll receive love, feedback, camaraderie, prayer, and accountability. It could be a home group, a Bible study, a men's or women's group, a twelve-step group such as Celebrate Recovery. Just make sure it's a Christ-centered small group. One that recognizes that the "higher power" is Jesus Christ.

The power of a small group is nothing short of amazing. The individuals in your small group will become important members of your support team.

An Attorney

Find a reputable family law attorney who can advise you in the area of finances. Consult the attorney in secret. In the confrontation step, just about every abusive husband will attempt to control and punish his wife by cutting her off from the money. You must know your legal rights and be prepared to protect yourself and the children when he squeezes you financially.

You will not confront your husband until you are emotionally and financially ready.

Speaking of money, you need to take steps now to be financially secure. Your husband may change, but if he doesn't, it is very likely that you will be on your own. During separation, or after a divorce, abusive husbands are not known for their generosity with money. Leaning on members of your support team, start preparing to take care of yourself and your kids.

Get more education. Get technical training for a specific career. Get a job. Get a new job with better pay and benefits. Ideally, you will have your own steady source of income—that you control—before you confront your abusive husband. This way, when he shuts off the money, it will be painful but not devastating.

STEP THREE: GET YOUR WORK DONE

To move successfully through my Escape from Abuse plan, you will require a wise and experienced coach. This will be a person who understands the dynamics of an abusive relationship and has guided many women through the escape process. This will be a person who can help you do three very important things: figure out why you have tolerated the abuse, heal from your unresolved past pain, and become an emotionally healthy woman who will stay in a marriage only when her husband treats her in a loving and respectful way.

This person will be a Christian counselor. He or she may be a psychologist or a master's level therapist. Here's the profile of the counselor you are looking for: a committed Christian who attends church weekly, is licensed in the mental health field (psychology, mental health, or marriage and family therapy), experienced in working with abused spouses, and a strong and assertive person who agrees with my Escape from Abuse plan.

To stand up to your husband and insist on dramatic changes in his treatment of you, you must first become emotionally healthy. An emotionally healthy woman does not tolerate being abused. To become healthy, you need to grapple with the roots of your enabling behavior: unresolved pain in your family of origin, in your personal life, and/or in previous romantic relationships.

If your father abused your mother, you are programmed to be a passive enabler and you'll be drawn to abusive men. Your dad's abuse of your mother may have been dramatic and obvious (as in physical violence, alcoholism or drug abuse, or vicious verbal attacks), or it may have been subtler (as in neglect or in controlling behavior, or always having to be right).

During your childhood, you may have been emotionally or sexually abused by your father or stepfather, grandfather, uncle, brother, stepbrother, neighbor boy, or another male. You may have been raped as a teenager or young woman.

You may have had a series of boyfriends who rejected you or who controlled you or verbally abused you. You may have allowed, perhaps because of low self-esteem, a boyfriend or boyfriends to have sex with you.

If I could talk to you for thirty minutes, I'd know exactly what in your past causes you to consent to the abuse your husband dishes out. This is what your Christian professional counselor will do. With his or her guidance, you will be able to work through your past pain and move forward as a new woman and a new wife.

Your Christian therapist will also assess your children and help make sure they are able to cope effectively with the escape process. What you tell the children—and when—about the abuse and the steps you are taking against it will depend on their ages, levels of maturity, and personalities. They may already be aware of some things.

Your children need to know the truth about the abuse and what it is costing you and them. They need to know what you are doing to escape it. They need to be emotionally ready before you confront your husband. Your Christian therapist will help you and the kids build toward becoming emotionally prepared for this final tough-love step.

If your husband is aware that you're going for counseling, tell him it is for you and your issues. He's not invited—not yet—and you will not tell him what you are actually doing in counseling. Most likely, he'll be fine with your going for counseling alone, because he's convinced that you're the one with the problems and that you are at fault for any marital issues. If he complains about the money for counseling, tell him *you are worth it*. If he refuses to pay, go to your support group and ask for their help to acquire the money you need.

STEP FOUR: GET INTO BIBLICAL TOUGH LOVE MODE

Once you have completed the first three steps—which may take several months—you are ready to confront your husband. It's time.

Before I describe the tough love steps, I want you to think about how your husband is likely to react. Here are the ten most common reactions by an abusive husband when his wife confronts him:

1. He'll be angry. "How dare you talk to me like that!" "I've done nothing wrong!" "It's your fault!"

2. He'll make promises, promises, promises. He'll plead, usually in tears, for a chance to change. "I'll do anything."

3. He'll ignore you. He'll shut down all communication and give you the silent treatment.

4. He'll try to get the children to be on his side and turn against you. "Mommy is being mean to Daddy." "Mommy is trying to kill our family." If he can get the children against you—make you the bad guy and on his side—this would be a big emotional weapon for him.

5. He'll cut you off from the money. He'll remove your name from the accounts and take away your credit and debit cards.

6. He'll try to get others (family, friends, pastor) on his side. He'll blame you for the marital problems and lie about your behavior. He'll start a smear campaign to destroy your reputation. "She's mentally unstable." "She's a psycho." "She may be bipolar."

7. He'll make threats. "I'll leave and never come back." "I'll take the kids and never come back." "I'll get custody of the kids." "I'll kill myself." "I'll quit my job so there will be no money." Any of these can be extremely effective with the kids if they have not been thoroughly prepared.

8. He'll attempt to buy you off. He'll buy things—car, clothes, jewelry, flowers, trips—to get you to back off and stay in your doormat role.

9. He'll play the martyr. "After all I've done for you, how can you be so ungrateful?" "Don't you remember all the good times?" "I work hard. I bought this home and your car and vacations. . ."

10. He'll claim he has changed. He'll be on his best behavior for a few weeks, maybe a month, and try to convince you he's all better.

Expect him to trot out one or more of these reactions. Ignore these bogus attempts to avoid real change and stick to the steps I describe below.

What Do You Do with a Sinner?
Your husband's abusive behavior makes him a sinner. A serious sinner. Here's what the Bible tells us to do with a serious sinner:

> *"If your brother sins, go and show him his fault in*
> *private; if he listens to you, you have won your brother.*
> *But if he does not listen to you, take one or two more*
> *with you, so that BY THE MOUTH OF TWO OR THREE*
> *WITNESSES EVERY FACT MAY BE CONFIRMED. If he*
> *refuses to listen to them, tell it to the church; and if he*
> *refuses to listen even to the church, let him be to you*
> *as a Gentile and a tax collector."*
>
> MATTHEW 18:15–17

God wants you to confront your abusive, sinning husband

the Matthew 18 way. But here is an important caveat: if your spouse is physically abusing you (and I would say that even one episode is extremely serious), I want you to put a direct confrontation on hold, leave your home as soon as you possibly can, tell the members of your support system the truth, and ask for help in finding a place to stay and for financial assistance. Take the kids and leave. Do not tell your husband where you are or where you are going. Call the police and get a restraining order. (Be aware, however, and on your guard, because restraining orders are easily and often violated.) Enlist the assistance of one or more of your support team to help you follow through with the confrontation steps below.

If you leave your home because of physical abuse, you will have your support team members perform the following confrontations. You personally will not be anywhere near your husband until he proves real change. In cases of physical abuse, he should face criminal charges, complete an anger management group, and go through at least three months of individual therapy before you will consent to joining him in marital therapy. The separation will continue until you have completed marital therapy and you are 100 percent confident that he can control his anger—that he will never physically harm you again.

Confront Him Three Times
Gather your support team, and tell them where you are in the process and that you are ready to confront your husband. Read Matthew 18:15–17 out loud, and pray together that God will use these steps to break your husband's heart and will and cause him to genuinely confess and repent. Ask your team to pray for you during each of the coming confrontations.

Next, go to your husband and schedule a meeting. Make sure the kids are out of the home when the meeting takes place. At the meeting, tell him he has abused you and exactly how he has abused you. Inform him that his continuing mistreatment of you makes him a sinner. Tell him you are going to follow the Bible and confront his sin. Read him Matthew 18:15–17.

Tell him that if he wants to continue living with you, he will need to complete four important action steps. Make it clear that all four are nonnegotiable. Read him the list, and then give him a copy:

1. You will see a Christian psychologist/therapist of my choosing. (It will probably be the same therapist you have been seeing.) We will both go to the first session so that I can make sure you tell the counselor the truth. You will go to two months of individual therapy and work on your abuse problem. You will sign a release so I can get regular updates from the therapist.
2. You will meet with our pastor (and again we'll both be at the first meeting), and he'll develop a spiritual growth program you will follow for two months. It will include weekly church attendance, a small group Bible study, a men's support group (such as Celebrate Recovery), and one-on-one discipleship with a godly man in the church. You will continue the support group and discipleship relationship for at least one full year.
3. You will find a godly man to serve as your account-ability partner. This could be the same man with whom you develop the one-on-one discipleship rela-tionship. You will meet this man face-to-face at least once a week. You will have an accountability partner for the rest of your life.
4. For two months, you will work hard on understand-ing the sources of your abusive behavior and ways to eliminate it. You will tell me everything that happens in your therapy. You will tell me everything that happens in your spiritual growth program. You will remain humble and very sorry for the damage you have done to me.

Tell him that if he follows through on these behaviors and shows real progress after two months, then and only then will you begin to respond favorably to him. You will agree to a marital session in which the therapist will lay out the game plan. It will probably be a combination of continued individual work for him and couples counseling for both of you. In the couples counseling, first you will heal from the damage his abuse has caused. Then the two of you will begin the process of building a new, beautiful, and fulfilling marriage.

Close this first meeting by informing your husband that you're giving him one week to think and pray about his sin and the pain it has caused you and decide whether he wants to follow these four requirements. Make it clear that if he acknowledges his sin (1 John 1:9) and proves to you his heartfelt desire to repent—that is, *change* how he treats you—you won't take any of the other Matthew 18 steps. But if he chooses not to repent, you will go on to the next step described in Matthew 18:15–17.

If he shows no sign of repentance after one week, quickly gather one or two of your closest friends/family members/supporters and take them with you to confront him again. Do not stall. Move forward quickly and decisively. You have waited long enough for your husband to change. Do not give him any warning that you are going to the next step in the process. This is a surprise attack. Just show up.

Ideally, one of your witnesses will be a man who knows your husband well. Let this man, or another member of your intervention group, do the talking. The point is to have another person deliver the same message that you gave to your husband when you initially confronted him: "You are sinning. You need to repent and take action to genuinely change as a husband. You have one week to show your wife—and us—that you're serious about changing and to agree to do the four action steps."

If, after another seven days, he remains in his sin, go immediately to your pastor and the leaders of your church. Take your Matthew 18 witnesses, your intervention group, with you. Explain to your pastor and church leaders, in detail, the pitiful state of your marriage, how your husband is sinning against you and God, and the steps you've already taken to bring him to repentance. If you have already told your pastor the truth, I hope he will be on board with the Matthew 18 intervention. Tell the leaders that you have already moved through the first two confrontations required by Matthew 18. Urge them to form a team and to go quickly to your husband to intervene.

Don't be shocked if your church leaders fail to follow through and deal with your husband. Many pastors and church board members will not agree with the assertive, tough love action you're taking. They'll ask you to be patient and submissive—which means continue to be abused because they're choosing not to deal with the problem. They'll tell you that if you just love him enough, he'll change. They may even blame you for your marriage problems. They may respond as if you are the sinner and that you could save the marriage if you would change.

Don't hold your breath waiting for the church leaders to confront your husband. In addition to their not agreeing with my approach, it's very likely they don't have the guts to confront an abusive man. Confrontation is tough, and many church leaders avoid doing it. There are some church leaders who will confront sinners and follow through with church discipline, but there aren't many. If your leaders haven't completed the intervention within three weeks, move on to the next step in God's Matthew 18 plan.

Shun Him

Your husband has weathered three interventions—or two, if your pastor and his team choke in the clutch and do nothing—and he isn't about to budge from his sin. Your job now is to shake him as he's never been shaken before in his life. You're at the end of the Matthew 18 process and will immediately and without any discussion "let him be to you as a Gentile and a tax-gatherer" (Matthew 18:17). You won't divorce him. I never recommend divorce. But you will shun him (which I describe in detail below). If that doesn't break him, you will physically separate from him.

As you begin your shunning, gather the children and tell them exactly what you're doing and why. Ask your therapist for guidance before you talk with the children. Tell them that Daddy is sinning by treating you badly. Give them specific, age-appropriate examples of his mistreatment. Explain what you have done in your attempts to try to change him. You have already told them some truth about their father, so this won't come as a complete shock to them. Read the Matthew 18 passage, and describe the interventions you've followed in obeying God's Word. Let them know that you'll be shunning their father in an attempt to force true repentance. Be clear that if he doesn't respond to the shunning, you'll be taking steps to separate from him. At the same time, continually assure them of your love and their security, and of God's presence and guidance.

Shunning means that, for one full month, you will ignore your husband. You will act as if he doesn't exist. You will talk with him only when absolutely necessary (such as an emergency situation). Move out of the bedroom. Provide him no services of any kind. No communication. No "Good morning," no "How was your day?" no "Good night." No time together at all. No food preparation for him. No laundry for him. No sex. You don't sit with him in church. You don't sit with him at your children's school or sporting events. For one full month, he doesn't exist.

If he's stupid enough to ask why you're doing this, ignore him. He knows why you're doing it. You are obeying the Bible and creating a crisis in his life. He needs to see that he has lost you. You've had it. You're over him and his sin, his terrible treatment of you.

Will he miss you? Will he want you back? Will he agree to the four actions? You'll see. A stubborn, sinful husband will change only when he realizes he has lost his wife. This is the moment of truth. Because of your courage, you have brought him to the brink.

If, after a month of shunning, he still remains in his sin, make your preparations to physically separate. Tell your children what you are doing and why. Break your silence by asking him to move out and leave the home. If he refuses or is obviously stalling, move out with the children. If you can't afford to move out or you have no place to go, stay at home and continue to shun him (but talk to your support group and ask them for help in finding a place to move with the kids).

If at any point in the Matthew 18 confrontation process your husband shows signs of breaking and repentance, be wary and stay pulled back. Do not jump back into his arms. Talk and promises are cheap. You require *action*. If he says he's ready to change, tell him to start by doing the four behaviors described above, and that you will be watching him.

WHAT IF HE REFUSES TO CHANGE?

Good question. I believe only God has the answer. I never recommend divorce. That's between you and God. Separation is as far as I go. I believe that separation, combined with the process I'm describing here, can save a marriage. If you follow scripture and pray for God's will, He will guide you and will show you what He wants you to do.

FOLLOW ABIGAIL'S EXAMPLE

Abigail, with God's help, confronted Nabal and let the chips fall. She was prepared for whatever response Nabal would give her. She drew a line in the sand—and even if Nabal had lived, she was forever changed. She would have tolerated no further abuse.

God took care of Abigail and her family. He'll take care of you and your family.

1. What are your fears about following my four-step Escape from Abuse plan? What would stop you from taking these steps? Share your fears and the potential obstacles with someone close to you whom you can trust.

2. Picture two scenarios: your life and your children's lives if you stay and do nothing versus your life and your children's lives if you follow my plan and take action against your abusive husband. Share these two scenarios with someone you trust, and ask that person to share how she sees the two scenarios playing out.

3. Identify your support team members. Over the next month, contact them and form your team.

4. Over the next month, find a Christian therapist and schedule your first appointment.

5. Commit right now to do the following four things over the next two weeks: (1) Read 1 Samuel 25; (2) pray and ask God if He wants you to follow my Escape from Abuse plan; (3) ask a close friend or family member and your pastor to read chapters 17 and 18 of this book; and (4) ask these two people in a face-to-face meeting if they believe you should follow the escape plan.

PART THREE

THE GOOD

The Proverbs 31 Wife
and Her Husband

OUTRAGEOUS SUCCESS
AS A COUPLE

19
A Beautiful, Two-Way Relationship

It's very easy to resent people who have what you want. Jealousy is petty, but it is also part of our fallen human nature. If someone has something you desperately desire to have, you hate that person. Well, *hate* may be a little strong, but you certainly have a very negative vibe for that person who has the nerve to possess what you crave.

You want so badly to be pregnant. You've been trying for months with no success. Whenever you go out, every third woman you see is pregnant. Why? It's not fair!

Your close friend drives up in a gorgeous, brand-new car. It is shiny, sleek, and state of the art. Even the color is striking. You are driving a car that is one stop from the junkyard. It is old, shabby, and on the verge of a major breakdown. And it smells bad. Two of your gauges don't work. The paint is badly faded. Your only consolation is that no one will ever steal it.

Several family members and friends have beautiful homes. Unbelievable curb appeal. New appliances, lovely furniture, and lush landscaping. Your home is the one the television makeover experts demolish and replace with a showpiece structure. When you arrive at other people's homes, you have to smile and say, "I just love your wonderful home." You'd like to yell, "You're living in a palace, and I'm living in a decrepit old dump!"

You are not happy in your marriage. You haven't been happy for a while. You have a friend who is very happy, almost too happy, in her marriage. She literally glows when she talks about her husband. They really seem to be soul mates. They're affectionate. They enjoy spending time together. They're in love. You want to be happy for them, but it's hard, because you yearn for that kind of marriage.

DON'T RESENT. . .LEARN

The truth is, we ought to be happy for those whom God is blessing. Especially married couples who are doing well in their relationships. They are not to be blamed for their lives going well for them. In many cases, these couples are doing things right and reaping God's rewards.

Up to this point, we have learned a lot from biblical couples making terrible mistakes. We've looked at couples who make good and bad decisions, and couples who make only bad decisions. Avoiding their mistakes is part of building a great marriage. But now it's time to learn from a biblical couple doing everything right.

The Proverbs 31 wife and her husband make only good, godly decisions. The twenty-two verses in this section (vv. 10–31) describe a spectacular relationship. No negatives are mentioned. Not one. It's all positive.

Let's not be threatened by this couple's success and happiness. Let's not resent what they have. Let's learn from what they do right. That's what God wants us to do. That's why their story is in the Bible.

I'll start with the wife, who is the main attraction in this passage. She builds three healthy relationships that give her the title of "an excellent wife" (31:10).

HER RELATIONSHIP WITH HERSELF

The Proverbs 31 wife is an emotionally healthy woman with a very positive self-image. She is strong, hardworking, and energetic (v. 17). She is dignified, assertive, and confident (v. 25).

She is a wise teacher and a kind, loving person (v. 26).

As a clinical psychologist, I see a woman who has a robust love for herself, based on her knowledge of God's love for her. Her confidence and adequacy come from *God* and not from herself (v. 30). She nurtures herself. She cares for herself. One of the foundational sources of her love for herself is her variety of outside-the-home interests. While she is clearly focused on her home and meeting the needs of her husband and children (vv. 15, 18–19, 21–22, 27–28), she has a rich life outside the home.

Five of the twenty-two verses are about her life in the outside world. She gathers materials to weave and sew, and she enjoys this work (v. 13). She shops and brings home unusual and interesting items (v. 14). She buys property, makes investments, and plants a vineyard (v. 16). She does volunteer work with the poor and the needy (v. 20). She has a home business and sells her products in the marketplace (v. 24).

She draws energy, vitality, and self-esteem from what she does in the outside world. She has a life of her own, and all her outside interests make her a better wife and mom. These verses make it clear that her outside activities do not detract from her home. Not at all! They enhance and enrich her home.

Wife, I recommend that you follow this wife's example and build a healthy life outside your home. I am convinced that the Proverbs 31 wife would heartily approve of three key actions.

First Action: Personal Time

Get personal time outside the home on a regular basis (without the kids). I call this the Great Escape. Actually, it's the Great Escapes—plural—because you have to do it over and over. Most women, single or married, focus on the home and everything that needs to be done there. The trouble is that the jobs are never done. They keep coming! You've just done four loads of laundry when you notice a new pile of dirty clothes in the laundry basket. Arrh! You've just vacuumed the living room rug and put the vacuum cleaner away, and when you walk back into the room you see crushed crackers and cookie crumbs on the rug! No!

It's hard for you to relax when there are jobs to be done, right? Your husband doesn't notice or may not care if there are a thousand jobs undone. But you care. So, to truly relax, you must get out of there.

By personal time, I mean doing something that's fun for you. Grocery shopping doesn't count. Going to the discount retailer to buy things for the kids doesn't count. Those are *jobs*. And they're done for *somebody else*. Your husband may think these count as time for yourself, but they don't. Do not use your personal time for jobs and errands.

Here are some examples of personal time:

- a fun shopping (or window shopping) trip
- lunch or dinner with a friend
- a Bible study
- going to a craft show
- going to the beach

You can do your activities alone or with a friend or two. It's your time, doing what you want to do. It's not for anyone else. It's for *you*.

I recommend that you get away for two or three hours *once a week*, perhaps using one weekday evening or part of a Saturday. Once a month, get away for half a day or a full day. Once a year, get away for an entire weekend. These times could be alone or with one or more girlfriends. *Schedule* these times, or they won't happen.

If you're married, make it clear to your husband that this is what you need. You'll have to approach him. He won't come to you and say, "Honey, I think you need regular personal time out of the home." Tell him, "This personal time will give me more energy, and it will help me be a better sex partner." That last one will get his attention.

Your husband may encourage you to take time away, but then he'll say, "But who's going to watch the kids?" You'll say, "I don't know, honey. Who can watch our kids? It's either you or me, and since I'll be gone, I guess that leaves you."

Your main obstacle to getting away will be *you*. You'll feel guilty. You'll feel selfish. You'll think, *There's no way I can leave! There are jobs to be done. The kids have needs. I don't want to get behind.*

I once met with a woman who was on the verge of major clinical depression. She was at her limit. She had small kids, worked outside the home, and had no time for herself. We worked out a deal: she was going to the beach for the weekend. Her husband was on board—not enthusiastically, but on board. Just before the planned weekend, she told me, "I'm not going to go." My response to her was, "You've chosen to go into a major depression, and it's your own fault."

Like so many women I've seen in therapy, this woman was functionally depressed. She was getting through life and handling all her many tasks, but she was exhausted and unhappy. Unless you want to be tired, burned out, and depressed, get out of the house on a regular basis. Do it with or without your husband's support. He may or may not understand the seriousness of your need. If he refuses to help with the kids, trade child care with friends or hire a babysitter. If you're a single mom, ask for help from your church. There are good people who will care for your children as a ministry.

God does not want you to crash and burn. He wants you to love yourself as He loves you, and to nurture yourself so that you can follow His plan for your life. His plan is not for you to be tired, burned out, and depressed. That's Satan's plan for you.

Second Action: A Hobby

Every woman needs an interest or activity that's fun. Something that gets you away from all the jobs you have to do at home. Something that reduces your stress and rejuvenates you. Perhaps more important, something that nurtures your personhood. When you're doing your activity, you're not an employee. You're not a mom. You're not a wife. You're not a daughter. You're not a grandmother. You are *you*. You're doing something that you like to do, and it expresses who *you* are.

You may do your fun activity during your personal time. That's fine and a good time-management strategy. It can be anything, but here are a few ideas to consider:

- scrapbooking
- sewing
- crafts
- shopping
- making stained glass or pottery
- painting
- taking a class
- reading
- playing a sport—golf, tennis, swimming
- jogging or walking
- going to the theater
- going to the beach or park

Don't say to me, "I don't have the time." *Make* the time. Do your fun activity at least once every two or three weeks. More often, if possible. It will meet some important needs.

Third Action: Regular Exercise
Consider these facts:

- Fact: Your body is the temple of the Holy Spirit (1 Corinthians 6:19–20), so it's important to take care of it.

- Fact: After the age of eighteen, we all go downhill physically unless we exercise regularly. If, after the age of twenty-five, we do not follow a regular exercise program, it's also true that we gain weight with virtually no limit.

- Fact: You must exercise regularly if you want to stay physically, emotionally, and spiritually healthy.

These facts aren't earth-shattering news. You're not thinking, *Exercise? Wow! I've never heard this before.* You know it's important to exercise. You just have to do it. Forget your lame excuses. Make the time and get it done.

The experts recommend exercising for thirty minutes three times a week. This is moderate exercise. You don't have to kill yourself. You're not training for the Olympics. You can walk, jog, or swim. There are all kinds of torture—I mean *exercise*—machines you can use at home: stationary bike, treadmill, rowing machine, cross-country skiing machine, StairMaster. You might even have one or more of these already. Perhaps they're in museum-quality condition because you never use them!

HER RELATIONSHIP WITH HER HUSBAND
The Proverbs 31 wife does *everything she can* to meet her husband's needs.

The heart of her husband trusts in her, and he will have no lack of gain (v. 11).

Her husband trusts her completely. Her careful management of the household brings in extra possessions and wealth.

She does him good and not evil all the days of her life (v. 12).

She supports him. She encourages him. She helps him. She consistently meets his needs.
She is happy in her marriage. Satisfied. Fulfilled.

Strength and dignity are her clothing, and she smiles at the future (v. 25).

She is strong. She is worthy of honor and respect by the way she lives. She is an impressive woman. She faces the future with total confidence. This must mean, in part, that her husband is meeting her needs. There's no way she is this happy and content if he is not treating her very well.

Why is he meeting her needs? I believe a key reason is found in verse 26:

> She opens her mouth in wisdom, and the teaching of kindness is on her tongue.

This is a confident, assertive, smart woman who has no problem speaking the truth. To anyone. Including her husband. Especially her husband. I believe she kindly and firmly makes her needs clear to him.

Here Are My Needs. . .Please Meet Them

I believe God wants you to speak the truth about your needs to your husband. It's his job to meet a certain number of your emotional, physical, and spiritual needs. That doesn't mean he's *going* to meet your needs, but he's supposed to. During courtship, he seems to meet your needs. After marriage, there can be serious drop-off in need meeting.

There are three things I want you to understand about your man:

- First, even a great husband will meet about 30 percent of your daily needs. That's it! Thirty percent. So don't look to him for any more than that.
- Second, he doesn't have a clue about how to meet your needs. If he's a typical husband, it's a safe bet that he's meeting a lot less than 30 percent of your needs. He tends to think of himself and has the intuition of a tree stump.

He'll pass by an overflowing laundry basket one hundred times without ever noticing or without it ever occurring to him that he could—actually—do the laundry. If he does notice, he'll say, "Hey, you need to do the laundry. I'm down to one pair of briefs."

You want to say, "No, you're down to one brain cell. Why don't *you* do a load of laundry?"

He'll watch television or be on the computer as you do job after job all around him: dishwashing, vacuuming, homework with the kids, dusting, laundry. Not once will he offer to help. It never dawns on him. He's in his own little world.

You say, "It sure would be nice to go out this weekend. You know, just the two of us." You say it right to his face.

He'll say, "Yeah, I guess it would." What's the matter with him? The answer is simple: He's a man! Any kind of subtlety is lost on a man. Another woman—especially a friend—would instinctively know your needs. Not your man. No way. A man requires direct, clear communication, or he won't get the message.

- Third, to get him to meet your needs, you must tell him exactly what your needs are.

  Ask him to take you out on a date once a week.
  "Honey, I'd like to go on a date once a week. Let's choose Saturdays. This Saturday I'll plan the date, and next Saturday you'll plan the date, and so on."

  Ask him to do certain chores.
  Discuss the exact chores you want him to do and reach an agreement. Write down the chores and post them. This will avoid your nagging him. "Honey, I don't want to nag you."

  Ask him for a daily Couple Talk Time.

"Honey, I want to have half an hour every day to talk with you. Let's do it at 8:30 pm, right after the kids go to bed."

Ask him to pray with you.
"Honey, I'd like us to pray together for five minutes three times a week. Let's pray before our Couple Talk Times on Monday, Wednesday, and Friday. Does that sound okay?"

Ask him to approach you in a certain way for sex.
Be gentle but specific. "Sweetheart, I can't respond well when you spring the idea of sex on me unpredictably. Please ask for sex in advance the day before or at least the morning of so I can be prepared. Even better, let's sit down each weekend and schedule our sex times."

It's a good idea to actually sit down and write a letter to him describing in detail your needs. Then schedule a meeting and read it to him. Ask him to tell you and write you *his* needs. Have a series of meetings in which you nail down specific strategies to meet needs.

Being this direct and specific with your needs won't guarantee that he'll meet them. But at least you'll have a chance. You probably think your man knows what your needs are. He doesn't. You probably think you communicate your needs clearly to your man. You don't.

Do what the Proverbs 31 wife does: assertively speak the truth about your needs to your husband. If he's a good man and he loves you, he will come through when he knows your needs.

HER RELATIONSHIP WITH GOD
Here is the real secret to the Proverbs 31 wife's happy, fulfilled life and marriage:

Charm is deceitful and beauty is vain, but a woman who fears the LORD, she shall be praised (v. 30).

It is no surprise that this verse comes right at the end of her story. God wants you to remember that He is the One who makes this extraordinary wife's life so rich and full. The health of all her relationships—with herself, her husband, and her children—depends on the close relationship she has with God.

Without question, God is the best source for meeting your needs. You have spiritual needs that only God can meet. There is a personal God whom you can know intimately. He is the God of the Bible. He is the only God. He is the most wonderful, beautiful, powerful, and loving person in the universe. And He wants to be close to you. He wants to meet your most important needs.

Though I am focusing on wives here, these spiritual principles also apply to husbands:

> *Know God*
> Come to know God through His Son, Jesus Christ. If you believe that Jesus Christ died on the cross for your sins and that He rose from the dead, you are a Christian (1 Corinthians 15:3–4). You know God.

> *Walk with God*
> Every day, spend time with God. Talk to Him, and listen to Him in prayer. Be honest with God about your feelings and doubts and fears. Go ahead and vent to Him and ask Him all your questions. That's what He wants you to do. That's how true faith is built.

> *Read the Bible*
> Read a portion of the Bible every day. Take a verse or two, and after reading, meditate for a

few minutes on what you have read. Ask God to speak to you through His Word. Ask Him to give you the truths from His Word that you can use to replace your sinful, inaccurate thoughts.

Take God with You
Wherever you go, take God with you. Throughout the day, engage Him in an ongoing dialogue, talking to Him in your mind and then recalling Bible verses and passages you have read from the Bible to "hear" God. God can also, through the Holy Spirit, communicate with you through thoughts and ideas and messages in your mind. He can "speak" to you through events and other persons. Tell Him your feelings. Tell Him your thoughts. Ask Him for truth, wisdom, guidance, and strength. No matter how weak your faith may be, God loves you and wants to help you.

What about the Guy?

The star of these twenty-two verses is obviously the wife. She is the "excellent wife" of verse 10. But her husband is no slouch either. He is an excellent husband.

This husband does two things that enrich his marriage and meet his wife's needs.

He Trusts and Delegates

I've already quoted this verse, but it's worth repeating:

The heart of her husband trusts in her, and he will have no lack of gain (v. 11).

This speaks well of the wife, as we've seen. But it also speaks well of the husband. He has complete confidence in his wife. He respects her abilities. He trusts her totally. Based on this view of her and what she can do, he delegates the running of the household and side businesses to her.

She is his equal partner. He gives her tremendous freedom to make decisions concerning their home and children. He doesn't criticize her or micromanage her. He is a leader and respected man in the community (v. 23), but he asks her to use her gifts and talents to manage the most important and precious part of their lives: their home and their children.

He Values and Praises

This husband knows one of the keys to unlocking his wife's heart is making her feel loved and cherished. He values her highly and isn't afraid to tell her:

> Her children rise up and bless her; her husband also,
> and he praises her, saying: "Many daughters have done
> nobly, but you excel them all" (vv. 28–29).

Is this guy good, or what? What wife wouldn't melt if she heard these words? He values all she is doing for him and their children and their family. *But* he realizes that simply valuing her isn't enough. He verbally tells her how much he values her.

His praise is a powerful way to express his appreciation and his love for her. And he makes sure she knows that she is not only a great wife and mom, but that she is the greatest wife and mom in the world.

Follow this husband's God-directed, brilliant example. Praise your precious wife often, and use superlatives. She is the most beautiful woman alive. She is the best mom alive. She is the best household manager alive. Well, you get the idea.

If you continually trust her, delegate to her, value her, and praise her, she will be the happiest wife alive. And you will be the happiest husband alive.

1. Wife, what kind of personal time outside of the home do you take? Do you have a hobby? Do you have a regular exercise program? Take action in these important areas.

2. Are you making your needs clear to your husband—so clear that he can repeat them to you? Tell him your top three needs. Tell him what he can do this week to meet these needs. Be specific.

3. For both of you—have you established a personal relationship with God through placing your faith in Jesus Christ? If you have not begun this wonderful adventure, go back to chapter 2 to read again exactly how to begin your relationship with God.

4. If you know God personally, how close are you to Him? Are you attending church each week? Are you spending time with God every day? Are you reading and learning from the Bible regularly?

5. Husband, do you trust your wife and delegate to her? Do you criticize or micromanage her? Wife, share with him your view of his trust and delegation.

6. Husband, do you value and praise your wife? What is stopping you from doing this? Wife, share with him your view of how he values you and praises you. Husband, right now, give your wife a specific compliment in three areas: her physical beauty, her character, and what she does for you and your home.

Joseph and Mary

OUTRAGEOUS FAITH IN GOD

20
Live God's Adventure
for Your Marriage

Are you a star athlete in a high-profile sport? Then you are a hero in our twenty-first-century culture. Are you a star in the entertainment world? You are a hero. Are you an extremely successful businessperson who runs a major corporation? You are a hero. Are you famous because you are on a reality television show that chronicles your every thought, feeling, and action every day? You are a hero.

These are the apparent criteria for hero status in our culture.

The culture could care less about your moral and spiritual life. In fact, if you are a highly moral and spiritual person, you are a fuddy-duddy, a rigid Goody Two-Shoes. The culture could care less about your relationship stability. In fact, if you are in a long-term marriage and seem happy with your spouse, you are a boring loser. The culture could care less about your parenting ability. In fact, if your children have turned out well, you have wasted years of your life raising them. You could have been working outside the home, making money all those years.

I'm about to tell you something you already know. Or, at least, should know. The real heroes in our culture aren't flashy. Most of them don't have great wealth. Most of them are not extremely successful in the areas of sports, entertainment, or business.

The real heroes are the regular, decent, rank-and-file

followers of Christ who get up every day and do their best to love their spouses, love their kids, and love and serve God. Other than a fairly small circle of family, friends, and coworkers, no one knows their names.

But do you know what? God knows their names, and He loves them. He is impressed with them. He blesses them and uses them to expand His kingdom. These heroes actually do extraordinary things with God's power—even if the world doesn't notice.

A COUPLE OF REAL HEROES

Two of the real heroes in the Bible are Joseph and Mary, earthly parents of Jesus Christ. For reasons you are about to discover, they are the most outrageously good couple in the Bible. Their story is an amazing story of commitment, love, teamwork, and faith in God.

By following their example, you can be real heroes and build a marriage after God's own heart.

"I'M GOING TO BE THE MOTHER OF THE SON OF GOD?" (LUKE 1:26–38)

Mary lives in the city of Nazareth. She is a virgin, engaged to Joseph. By Jewish custom, she cannot have sexual intercourse with Joseph for one full year. After the year of waiting, they will marry and consummate their marriage and move in together as husband and wife.

The angel Gabriel comes to Mary and turns her life upside down. Gabriel tells her she will conceive and give birth to a son, whom Mary is to name Jesus. He will be the Son of God. And, oh, by the way, *the Holy Spirit will supernaturally bring about the conception of Jesus.*

The first shock for Mary: "I'm talking to an angel!" The second shock: "I will give birth to the Son of God!" The third shock: "Joseph will not impregnate me! The Holy Spirit will."

The fourth shock is the realization that her normal life is officially over. "No one, especially Joseph, is going to believe my story. It's ridiculous. It's absurd. It's impossible! Everyone will say it's the rambling of a crazy woman or a liar. Everyone will believe I've had sex with another man and am carrying his baby. Period. End of discussion. I will live in disgrace, and Joseph certainly will not marry me. No one will marry me."

Incredibly, Mary does not protest. She responds with instant obedience:

> Mary said, "Behold, the bondslave of the Lord; may it be done to me according to your word."
>
> LUKE 1:38

This is *an outrageous faith in God*. If this is what God wants, it's what Mary wants.

Gabriel ends his pronouncement with these words: "For nothing will be impossible with God" (Luke 1:37). Important words, because Mary and Joseph will face many impossible situations in the next few years of their marriage.

"WHAT DO YOU MEAN, YOU'RE PREGNANT?" (MATTHEW 1:18–19)

Joseph finds out that Mary, the love of his life, is pregnant, and he knows he's not the father. They are betrothed but not living together, because they're in that one-year-of-no-sex waiting period. His heart must be broken. He is probably angry and deeply hurt. His Mary has betrayed him. She has disgraced and humiliated him and has treated with contempt the faith in God she professes.

The logical and culturally prudent decision is to publicly reveal Mary's sin of having sex outside of marriage. This will save his reputation by making it clear to the Jewish community that he is not the father. Plus, Mary should have to face the severe consequences of her awful betrayal. Who could blame Joseph for wanting payback?

Instead, Joseph decides to do everything he can to protect Mary. Rather than expose her apparent sin of adultery, which could have resulted in her death by stoning, he decides to divorce her quietly. Though in terrible pain from her betrayal, Joseph still wants to shield Mary from public ridicule and threat of death.

This is *outrageous love for Mary*.

"YOU'RE MY WIFE, NO MATTER WHAT!" (MATTHEW 1:20–25)

In a dream, an angel tells Joseph that Mary has conceived through the Holy Spirit and that his son will be the Messiah (Matthew 1:20–21). The angel instructs Joseph to take Mary as his wife.

Wait just a minute! It is perfectly reasonable for Joseph to respond, "Do you know what you are asking me to do? In my Jewish culture, taking a wife who is carrying someone else's baby is not done. Ever! One hundred percent of Jewish men would never marry her. Very few people will believe the story that Mary conceived through the Holy Spirit. Frankly, it's hard for me to believe. This stigma will be on us and our family for the rest of our lives!"

But Joseph obeys God by instantly doing what the angel asks. He violates—shatters, really—Jewish custom by immediately taking Mary into his home instead of divorcing her or at least waiting out the one-year period of intercourse-free betrothal. He wants to obey God and take tender care of his wife. He doesn't care about the inevitable scandal and controversy in their tight-knit community.

This is *outrageous faith in God* and *outrageous love for Mary*.

"THIS IS BAD TIMING FOR A CENSUS!" (LUKE 2:1–5)

To comply with Caesar Augustus's census decree, Joseph and the very pregnant Mary have to travel from Nazareth to Bethlehem. As if they didn't already have enough problems.

It is a seventy- to ninety-mile journey. It is over rugged terrain. Joseph is on foot, and Mary is on a donkey. They will have to sleep outside, in the elements, along the way. Mary is at the critical, late stage of her pregnancy.

The trip is not only not ideal, it is brutal, exhausting, and dangerous.

Joseph and Mary do not even flinch. They gear up and go through this ordeal together.

This is *an outrageous commitment to each other*.

"DON'T TELL ME THERE'S NO ROOM AT THE INN!" (LUKE 2:6–7)

They finally arrive in Bethlehem with Mary on the verge of giving birth to Jesus. With the way their lives are going, they should not be surprised that there are no rooms available at the Bethlehem Inn.

Mary gives birth to Jesus in a stable. This is a place where livestock feed. It is terribly crude. It is horribly unsanitary. It is barely sheltered from the weather. It is an unbelievably inappropriate location for God's only Son to be born.

No mom to help with the delivery of the baby. No family and friends to help with the newborn. It's just Joseph and Mary. But that's all they need: each other.

This is *outrageous teamwork in their marriage*.

"WE HAVE TO RUN FOR OUR LIVES?" (MATTHEW 2:13–15)

With Jesus now a child, an angel warns Joseph in a dream to take Mary and Jesus and escape to Egypt. The wicked and powerful King Herod is seeking to find and kill Jesus.

Talk about terrifying. Beyond stressful. Seriously traumatic. In an attempt to kill Jesus, this wicked man ordered the slaughter of all the male children two years old and younger in Bethlehem and environs. In his lifetime, he had family members and foes killed. The child Jesus was in acute and immediate danger. If Herod wanted you dead, you became dead.

There is no complaining recorded at all. Joseph obeys God, and he and his young family flee to Egypt. What's another move? What's a desperate run from the most notorious and bloodthirsty madman in the land?

This is *an outrageous faith in God*.

"If God Tells Me to Go, I'll Go" (Matthew 2:19–23)

Joseph has two more dreams. In one, an angel tells him Herod is dead and to return to Israel. In the second dream, God Himself warns Joseph not to return to Bethlehem, but to set up residence in Nazareth. Archelaus, one of Herod's sons, is now the ruler over the area that includes Bethlehem, and he is just as unstable and murderous as his father.

Again, this is a very scary time for Joseph and Mary. Again, Joseph obeys God and does what he is told. He completely trusts in God and His ability to protect him and his small family.

This is *an outrageous faith in God*.

Lessons from Joseph and Mary

Joseph and Mary's story offers four simple but powerful lessons for you and your spouse. First, *have an outrageous commitment to your spouse, no matter what*. Obeying God means maintaining your sacred covenant of marriage. Your marriage is a legal contract, but it is much more than that in God's eyes. It is a permanent, lifelong covenant, a most serious *promise*.

Stay married, regardless of the obstacles that come your way. Do your absolute best to weather serious attacks on your marriage, from within and without. Despite enduring many serious obstacles, Joseph and Mary remain committed to each other.

Second, have *an outrageous love for your spouse*. There ought to be nothing undone on your list of things you want to do for your spouse. If your spouse has a need, your job is to do whatever you can to meet it. Even if it comes at great personal cost.

Joseph puts himself and his reputation at huge risk because of his love for Mary. He does not care about himself. He cares about Mary and what is best for her. That is true love.

Third, have *outrageous teamwork as a couple*. It is difficult and painful times that build your teamwork and your love for each other and for God. Joseph and Mary have a third member on their team: God. And God is at the center of their team.

Teamwork does not grow significantly when life is smooth. As a result of dealing with traumatic circumstances, Joseph and Mary become a terrific and close team. A team of *three*.

Fourth, have *an outrageous faith in God, as individuals and as a couple*. Believe that God has a plan, a good plan, for your marriage and family. God will always be faithful and show you what to do. Your job is to follow the path He reveals.

For Joseph and Mary, it is all about God and what He wants them to do. God will probably not speak to you personally or through angels, but He will show you what to do: through the Bible, prayer—individual and as a couple—godly counsel, and a process of thorough discussion of decisions.

It's time for the two of you to reap the rewards of outrageous commitment, outrageous love, outrageous teamwork, and outrageous faith in God. The rewards are:

- a closer and stronger marriage
- a closer personal relationship with God
- a closer relationship with God as a couple

And, best of all, you will experience the reward of living God's adventure for you as a couple.

A FINAL MESSAGE
Did you enjoy the ride with these ten outrageous couples of the Bible? I hope so. I know I did. These couples teach us many essentials we need to build wonderfully intimate and fulfilling marriages.

Avoid the awful mistakes these couples made. Emulate their great decisions and actions. Most of all, keep God at the center of your marriage. God is the source of your love. God is the source of your good decisions as a couple and as individual spouses. God is the source of your respect and trust for each other. God is the source of your spiritual and emotional and physical intimacy.

When you do marriage God's way, as illustrated by these couples, you will enjoy outrageous love, and you will live God's outrageous adventure for your marriage.

Outrageous Interaction

1. Talk about a difficult, stressful time in your relationship. What happened? What obstacles did you face? How did you get through it together? What was your reward?

2. Have you not yet recovered from a traumatic event in your relationship? Be honest. If you have not, agree now to see your pastor or a Christian therapist to start the healing process.

3. Do you have an *outrageous commitment* to each other? Will you stay married, no matter what? What would cause you not to stay committed?

4. Do you have an *outrageous love* for each other? Would you do anything, and I mean *anything*, to show your love for your spouse? Tell your spouse one action he or she can do that would show you an outrageous love.

5. Are you an *outrageous team*? With God's help, do you work together to get through painful times? How can you improve your teamwork?

6. Do you have an *outrageous personal faith in God*? What can you do individually to get closer to God? Do you have an *outrageous faith in God as a couple*? What can you do together to get closer to God as a couple?

About the Authors

David E. Clarke, PhD, is a Christian psychologist, speaker, and author of ten books, including *I Don't Want a Divorce*. A graduate of Dallas Theological Seminary and Western Conservative Baptist Seminary in Portland, Oregon, he has been in private practice for twenty-five years. He and his wife, Sandy, have four children and one granddaughter. They live in Florida.

William G. Clarke, MA, has been a marriage and family therapist and speaker for more than thirty years. He is a graduate of the University of Southern California and the California Family Study Center, where he earned his master's degree. With his wife, Kathleen, he served with Campus Crusade for Christ for nine years. He established the Marriage and Family Enrichment Center in Tampa, Florida, where he and Kathleen live.

Resources

Other books by David Clarke:

- *Men Are Clams, Women Are Crowbars: Understand Your Differences and Make Them Work*
- *A Marriage After God's Own Heart*
- *What to Do When Your Spouse Says, I Don't Love You Anymore: An Action Plan to Regain Confidence, Power, and Control*
- *I Don't Want a Divorce: A 90-Day Guide to Saving Your Marriage,* with William G. Clarke
- *Married but Lonely: Seven Steps You Can Take With or Without Your Spouse's Help,* with William G. Clarke
- *Parenting Is Hard and Then You Die: A Fun But Honest Look at Raising Kids Right*
- *I'm Not OK, and Neither Are You: The 6 Steps to Emotional Freedom*
- *Kiss Me Like You Mean It: Solomon's Crazy in Love How-to Manual*
- *Honey, We Need to Talk: Get Honest and Intimate in 10 Essential Areas,* with William G. Clarke
- *Enough is ENOUGH: How to Leave an Abusive Relationship*

To schedule a seminar, order Dr. Clarke's books, set up an in-person or telephone advice session, schedule a marriage intensive, or access his speaking schedule, please contact:

> David Clarke Seminars
> Marriage & Family Enrichment Center
> 6505 North Himes Avenue
> Tampa, FL 33614
> 1-888-516-8844
> www.davidclarkeseminars.com